The Secret of Uniball

The Secret of Uniball

Nihar Vyas

PRABHAT PRAKASHAN
ISO 9001: 2008 Publishers

Published by
PRABHAT PRAKASHAN
4/19 Asaf Ali Road,
New Delhi-110 002 (INDIA)
Tele : +91-11-23289777
e-mail: prabhatbooks@gmail.com

ISBN 978-93-86300-84-3
THE SECRET OF UNIBALL
by Nihar Vyas

Edition
First, 2017

Price
₹ 250.00 (Rupees Two Hundred Fifty only)

Cover Design by
Har Shiv Sharma

Printed at
R-Tech Offset Printers, Delhi

- ❖ For my grandfather, who is having tea with God.
- ❖ For my loving grandma, who encouraged me to write.
- ❖ And for my mom and dad, who helped me so much with this book.
- ❖ And my unforgettably mischievous sister Yashsvi, whose sharp comments helped me to keep writing.

Author's Note

I request all the readers to read this book as if you yourself are in the place of the hero. This will add both interest and a sense of adventure. This is my first book and I have written it with full enthusiasm, courage and hope that the readers will like it. I have complete trust that the readers will appreciate this book.

Now take a deep breath and get started for a journey of friendship, trust and courage!

Prologue

Five centaurs[1] were crawling down the stairs of a tall tower. They all were in the outfit of a warrior. Three of them had five horns in their hands. The fourth centaur was holding a sword and the fifth one was holding a camera.

One of them said, "We need to do this work fast and without any mistake."

"Yes, or else the commander will kill us!" The one holding a camera said.

"Don't be afraid! We'll complete this work!" The centaur said while holding the two horns.

They reached near a golden door and inserted a horn into a small hole. The door opened and they entered into it. The only light, which was filling the room, was coming from a glowing box. The centaur that was holding the sword opened the box. There was a hollow ball with blue smoke into it. The smoke stirred while the centaurs did their work.

The centaur that was holding the camera stood in front of the three centaurs. The three centaurs positioned their five horns in such a position, over that ball, that the tip of the horns met at the same point.

---

1. Origin Greek *Kentauros*: A creature with a man's head, arms, and upper body and a horse's lower body and legs.

Suddenly, the smoke in the ball stopped stirring. Then, a small thread, followed by a continuous energy, started transferring from the ball to the horns.

The centaur that opened the box took out a small container from the bag which he was carrying. He placed the container on top of those five horns. The energy first got into the horn and then into the cylindrical container. Then, the energy flow finished and got stored in the cylinder.

They finished the work. The centaur holding a camera took out a small mike and spoke into it, "Commander, the work is completed. You must've seen the recording. Should we run out of here?"

A voice said, "Yes, and come here fast!" The voice was as if two voices were speaking at the same time.

The centaurs got out of the room and ran up the tower. There were five small jetpacks there. They took them and glided out of the city. It was night time and the whole city was quiet. While they were getting out, another creature saw them. He was a unicorn.

He yelled, "You thieves, stop!" He rang a large bell and everybody in the city woke up.

The centaurs landed outside the walls of the city and one centaur spoke in his mike, "Sir, we've got out of the city and we're coming!"

Miles away, a creature was sitting in front of a large screen. He had seen everything that the camera had recorded and he had ordered the centaurs to come back quickly. He started laughing wickedly in his hideous voice.

The unicorn that had rung the bell ran to the tower. He entered into it and stopped on the eighth floor (the tower had ten floors).

He entered into a room. A very old unicorn got up from the ground and said in a calm tone, "What happened, Stan? Have any intruders entered in Florencia?"

The unicorn bowed and said, "Sir, five centaurs were spotted gliding outside Florencia with jetpacks. They looked like they were escaping from the city."

"You go and alert the guards. I'll go and see the Uniball!"

The younger unicorn ran outside the room. The older unicorn climbed upstairs towards the ninth floor. He entered into the room where that box was kept. He opened it and saw the ball inside. It looked fine.

He touched his horn to it and the horn went inside. After some time, he took out his horn. He looked worried.

Then the unicorn named Stan entered into the room. He asked, "What happened? Is everything fine?"

"No, the Uniball's power is stolen; a part of it is missing!"

"What? But how is this possible? The Uniball cannot be removed from its place, then how can those Centaurs steal it?" Stan asked.

"The Centaurs have become a lot powerful than they were the last time. They must have invented a technique through which they could steal this power!" The Prime Unicorn replied.

"What should we do now? Should we attack Centauria?" He suggested.

"No, no, that would be useless because the Centaurs have developed a lot during the last few years. They could easily outnumber us!" The Prime

Unicorn replied. "None of us have the power to defeat them. Their powers are in a much more advanced form than us!"

"Then, will Uniball's power be lost... forever?" Stan's face became more tensed.

The Prime Unicorn said nothing.

"So, should we believe that the evil and bad powers have won?"

...There was no answer.

❃❃❃

All the animals of Florencia were huddled together on the terrace of that tall tower (where the Uniball was kept). Everybody seemed in a state of shock and worry. There were animals, unicorns and humans too.

Stan was standing in the front. Behind him, two other unicorns were talking, "The Uniball's power was stolen last night. This means that we are weak now. After what happened with that...."

Before he finished his line, the Prime Unicorn came on the terrace. He looked in a good mood as he had a little smile on his face. Every creature present on that terrace bowed before him.

He said, "I thank all of you for coming here. I know that we are going through a hard time. The Uniball's power is stolen again and we don't have enough resources!"

"Then what should we do now? Are we completely defeated?" A human from within the crowd said."

"No, we are not defeated. I went deeper into the Uniball and searched the whole night. I have found something interesting. First, look at this."

His horn glowed and suddenly, a screen appeared in the sky. On it, two words were written – *Hindu Mythology*. After that, the scene shifted and another word was written – *Narsimha.*[2]

Then, there was a photo of a weird creature. He had the head of a lion and the rest of the body of a human. He was standing on the doorstep of a big palace. In his lap, lied a demon whose stomach was being cut by the nails of that creature. The Prime Unicorn started speaking –

"I wanted to tell you that there was a very ferocious demon called *Hiranyakashyap* in Indian myths? He had got the boon that he could not be killed by a god or a human or an animal. He could not die in morning or in night. His death could not happen by any weapon. He could not die inside his house or outside his house. He could neither die in the space nor on the earth."

Stan was amazed, "But how was he killed then?"

"Lord Vishnu then took an *Avataar*[3] of a beast called Narsimha whose head was of a lion and his body was that of a human. He came out of a pillar to kill the demon at the twilight (neither day nor night); on the doorsteps of his palace (neither inside nor outside); used his nails to kill (neither animate nor inanimate); put him on his lap before killing (neither on earth nor in space), thus making the power of the boon ineffective."

"Whoa, what an intelligent plan!" Stan said.

---

2. Narsimha: Origin Hindu Mythology; Half lion and half human. It was the fourth incarnation of Lord Vishnu to kill the demon Hiranyakashyap.
3. Avataar: The form taken by god to destroy evil. It could be in any form such as a human, an animal or a beast.

But what can we do with this information?" a unicorn standing beside Stan said.

"This story tells us that however big the evil is, someone in this world is created to destroy it. After the long night of research, I came to know that there is someone who could defeat those Centaurs. But..." The Prime Unicorn paused, then said, "...he would not be someone amongst us! He will arrive in a form that none of us would have ever thought of!"

"Really, but who is he?" Stan was shocked

"I don't know. I called all of you here in this meeting to tell you that all the hope has not yet been vanished. We can still win. Now, you all should go back and thanks again for coming here!" Everyone looked happy now.

"And Stan, please stay here for a few minutes." The Prime unicorn added.

When everybody had left, the Prime unicorn said, "The Uniball also told me that the time has arrived when we should call our savior. He has arrived in the outer world. He is very close to us. You go and keep an eye on whoever has just arrived in those farmhouses."

"...Or, you can bring any one of his personal things like a diary or anything", the Prime Unicorn said.

Stan nodded and left the room. The old unicorn was left thinking about the words which Uniball had told him – Your savior has arrived. Only he can save you. He is the one who is chosen and his name is... Parth!

Stan had kept a close eye on everyone in the farmhouses and when he noticed a kid who had recently arrived, he was not sure that this was the chosen boy. He went to Prime Unicorn and told him about this doubt.

"Sir, I think you are wrong somewhere as the person who has just arrived in the farms is an ordinary kid. How can he fight this big problem?" Stan presented his worry. He took out a diary. "I found nothing else. Yes, he always writes a diary which he brought from his homeland. Can it be of any use?"

The Prime Unicorn opened the diary and flipped some pages. He came across the dates 12, 13 and 14 April, 2013:

12 April, 2013

Today, grandma told me the story of 'Mahabharata'. Every character had a specific role to play in the story. The plot was also very cool. I was thrilled to know that Krishna, who was a god, became the charioteer of Arjun, a simple warrior. Arjun won at last, but a question lurks in my mind, who is greater: Krishna or Arjun?

13 April, 2013

I asked that question to grandma that between Krishna and Arjun, who is greater? She told me that everyone is special, but we need to have faith in ourselves. Krishna only lighted the way for Arjun and he defeated the evil 'Kauravas'.

14 April, 2013

Today, I also read the story of 'Ramayana'. In that story too, there was central character like Arjun, called Hanuman. He remembered and recognised his powers after the encouragement from 'Jamwant', the king of bears. This means that every person has some powers and he only needs to recognise them, cool!

The Prime Unicorn looked towards Stan with a small smile. Stan was still confused. The Prime Unicorn said, "Stan, Parth is our savior. Look at this diary. This is the proof!"

"But how can you be so sure?" Stan asked.

"In every era, a person is chosen who defeats the bad powers and saves the mankind. Look, this diary also shows that one only needs to recognise his powers and he proves to be special." He walked towards the edge of the tower. "The Uniball has planned something. Why else would Parth talk about recognising our powers? All this cannot be a coincidence!"

"Okay, now I understand. But what do we do till then?"

The Prime Unicorn stretched his gaze over the city and said, "Till then we must...*believe*!"

Contents

1
An Advice

"Sam, please can you stop running?" I called out to Sam but he wasn't listening. I ran faster to catch up with him. When I reached near him, he pointed towards our front and told me, "There are the fields."

I was behind Sam when I saw a big stone on the ground.

I warned Sam, "Sam, look out!" But I was late. He had already hurt his leg and was sitting on the ground making noises like "Oouch…Aaah!"

Sam and I had almost reached the fields when we had to turn back. I picked up his backpack, gave Sam my support and we started back. Sam was still groaning with pain. I thought it foolish of him to cry as we both were in ninth grade.

My name is Parth. I have a long face. My complexion is somewhat between fair and dark. I have black hairs and I prefer them long (keeping in the boundaries of a boy!). My eyes are brown and I have a tall height which I am proud of! I am very fond of books.

Here is my friend Sam who has hurt his leg. Sam's full name is Samuel Morris. He has brown hairs and light green eyes. Sam has a rectangular face and his height is same as my height.

Actually, when my summer holidays began, I had an invitation from my uncle to spend the holidays with him in Rome. The mythology of Rome always fascinated me and when I got the chance to go to Rome, I did not miss it. At first, my parents were not willing, but when they saw my urge to go there, they agreed.

When I had arrived here, the atmosphere did not look good to me. I felt something strange in my heart like something was missing. Then, when uncle Dhairya took me to all the good places of Rome, I ignored the feeling and eventually forgot it.

I went to places like Saint Peter's basilica, the Pantheon, the Colosseum, Palatine Hill, Vatican Museums and many other places. It looked as if the architectural structure of Rome is somewhat similar to India. Many churches and shrines had the same curved upper structures as were in India.

The surroundings in Rome are very religious as many churches and shrines are here. Indian culture and Roman culture have some similarities. Both of them have mythologies that represent each other in some aspect. For example, in Indian myths, we have Brahma, Vishnu and Shiva as the three prime gods. In Roman myths, Jupiter, Neptune and Pluto are the three main gods.

There are four main mythologies in this world – Indian, Greek, Roman and Egyptian. I had read many books about all these myths and knew a few things about them. Amongst them, my favorite was that of Rome as the gods here were very awesome.

Greek and Roman myths are almost the same but the difference is of names and that the gods were more peaceful in Greece. In Rome, the gods always went on fights and became angry faster.

I also made a lot of friends here with whom I played in the evening. Sam was my best friend in Rome. We had planned that we will come to these fields and spend some time here, but he got hurt and we had to return.

The way to the forests was towards our left. Just then I saw something white in the outer part of the forests. I thought that it might be some kind of white flowers but then it suddenly moved.

I said to Sam, "Sam, look what's that?" He grunted, "Unh?!" He was still groaning with pain. When I looked back, the light had disappeared.

We reached the farmhouses. They were settled towards both the sides of the road. The second farmhouse was of Sam's. I was still giving my support to Sam when we reached his farmhouse. I rang the bell and his mother opened the door. As soon as she saw Sam, she was worried.

Before I could say something, she said, "Sam! What happened? How did you get hurt?" I told her how Sam got hurt and we had to come back.

She said, "Oh! It was so thoughtful of you to help him but now you should go to your house. I'll look after him."

I reached my farmhouse and went in. Uncle Dhairya was sitting on a chair, reading a novel. He is a round and fat man with an affectionate smile. He has half bald head with some black and grey hairs. He got settled in Rome twenty-five years ago.

He asked, "Parth, why are you home so early?" I told him the full story of Sam getting hurt. After that, he said, "Oh! Poor Sam, he got hurt. How is he now?"

"I don't know. His mother said that she'll look after him."

Just then aunt Kshama came in. She is almost same as Uncle Dhairya, round and fat, but she has long brown hairs (obviously she will not be half bald, silly!).

She also questioned, "Have you explored the fields so early?"

I repeated the story once again. "Is he well now?" she asked.

"I think so."

Suddenly she said, "Oh goodness me, look at the clock. Parth you should have your lunch now."

"I have to go to the market also," she muttered.

She brought uncle Dhairya's and my lunch." Now you two, wash your hands and sit down to eat," she ordered us.

While eating, I asked Uncle Dhairya about the white light and how it disappeared in the forest.

He said, "Forget it. It could be a dove or a pigeon. We should now have our lunch or else your aunt will scold both of us."

We finished our lunch. Uncle Dhairya started reading his novel. Just then, the phone rang and I knew that it was of my mom. My parents had called me a thousand times since I arrived here. I wake up in the morning and find that my mom had called me a few minutes ago. During lunch, Dad's call is attended by me, followed by a hundred questions like 'Have you eaten your lunch?', 'Are you getting bored?', 'Is everything alright there?', and so on.

I went to Sam's house. He was feeling well. So, we came out and started to play catch-catch near my

Uncle's house. During playing, I told Sam about that white light but he also said that it could be a bird.

Suddenly, Sam threw the ball too far and it landed just inside our mysterious neighbor, Mr. Amerigo Clapperton's garage. I could never understand his name.

Sam gasped. He said, "What do we do now? That was my new ball. I don't think that man will give back our ball.

I said, "Don't worry. We both will go inside and if Mr. Clapperton comes, we'll tell him about our ball. Okay?"

Sam said uncertainly, "Um....Alright! But if anything happens, you will explain it to him."

"Okay! Can we now go in?"

We entered the garage and the sight which we saw inside was incredible. There were no cars or bikes but there were hundreds and thousands of books.

I took out one book. Its name was 'Unicorns – myths or reality'. I took out another book. It was also about Unicorns. Sam too found books only about Unicorns.

I said, "Strange...the books here, I think, are about Unicorns only."

Sam also agreed. There were toys, cards, key-chains, posters of Unicorns and many more. Our ball was in one corner of the garage. A table was also kept there. Some notes were kept on it and some mathematical calculations were also done on it. On one paper, there was written 'Uniball's power is stolen – 15 percent.'

Sam said to me, "I think Mr. Clapperton believes in all those fairytale stuff. I don't think that there is anything like Unicorns. Now we should take our ball and get...."

Before he could finish, a booming voice said behind us, "If you do not believe in the myths, you should."

Mr. Clapperton was standing right behind us. He is a tall man with small white beard and round glasses.

"What are you both doing here?" He continued.

I tried to explain, "Mr. Clapperton, our ball came here. So, we came to...."

He cut me short, "I don't want to hear anything. You both get lost from here."

Sam said, "But...."

"No arguments!" he said.

We came out. I said to Sam, "What's his problem? We only came to take our ball and he talked so rudely."

Sam said, "Now forget about him and catch this throw!"

"Yes," I said, but Mr. Clapperton's voice was still ringing in my ears, "If you do not believe in the myths, you should."

□

2

The Dream

The next day, I said to Sam, "Hey Sam, can we go to the library today?"

Sam agreed, "Yes! I know the way."

David, who was our other friend, said, "Hey, have you both forgotten us? We are also coming with you."

"Yeah you all can come," Sam said.

"Come on! First we will go to our houses, inform our parents, take our cycles and go to the library," I said to them.

Everybody cheered up and went to their homes. I went to my farmhouse and told Uncle Dhairya, "Uncle, we are going to the library. So I'll be late. Don't worry about me."

He said, "Okay! Go and enjoy."

I said, "I also need your bicycle."

"Oh, it's yours till you are here. Good bye."

I left the farmhouse and waited for my friends at the end of the road where farmhouses ended. When they all arrived, we started for the library which was in the city.

We spent the whole afternoon in the city and came back to the farmhouses when the sun was just about to set. I said, "Hey, tomorrow we will play Basketball in that court which is nearby. Okay?"

Everybody said 'yes' and went back to their farmhouses. When I entered the farmhouse, Uncle Dhairya was doing something with a lawn mower in the garage.

He said, "Oh, welcome back, Parth! You came on just the right time. Your Aunt has made the dinner and we were waiting for you."

We sat down on the dining table to eat. Just then I remembered the events of yesterday. I had not told uncle and aunt about Mr. Clapperton and his garage. I told them everything that happened in Mr. Clapperton's garage and his unusual advice.

"You should stay away from him," Uncle said. "He's got a high temper and is kind of a strange person."

Aunt Kshama added, "Yes, and I think he believes in all these myths like unicorns. Even after he is living here for 10 years, he has still got the air of a stranger."

"Anyway, forget him and eat your dinner," Uncle Dhairya finished the discussion and we had our dinner quietly.

After the dinner, I went to my room upstairs and made my bed. Just when I had finished making the bed, Aunt Kshama's voice came from downstairs, "Parth, switch off the lights."

I replied, "Yes, Aunt."

I switched off the lights and the moment I placed my head on the pillow, because of tiredness, I fell into a deep sleep.

I was walking in some kind of forest. Dry leaves were scattered on all over the path and were making crunching noises under my feet. I was going deeper into the forest. In the way I saw many plants and trees whose names I didn't remember or didn't know.

Suddenly, I heard distant hoof beats and had a feeling that whoever it was, was behind me. I looked back but no one was there.

When I looked in front, a Unicorn was standing there. I screamed and started to run.

Then, the Unicorn spoke, "Please stop, dear friend. I had no intention to frighten you."

His voice was calm and soothing. I stopped.

"I...I...I was n...not frightened but w...was startled," I stammered.

"I'm sorry," he said, "But our world needs you. We are in a big problem, Parth."

I asked, "How do you know my name?"

"The Prime Unicorn will help you to understand all this!" he replied.

Suddenly I woke up. "Was that a dream?" I said to myself, "What a weird one!"

I stood up from my bed to drink some water. While drinking water, I looked through the window.

'Hey, was there really a white light in the garage of our mysterious neighbour, Mr. Clapperton?' – I thought.

Just then, a strange, white, horse-like creature ran outside the garage and disappeared in the woods.

After him, Mr. Clapperton came out of the garage and went into his house. I looked at the clock hanging on the wall. 3.45 am. Why was he not asleep at this time? Was there any link between my weird dream and these strange events?

I tried to sleep but could not. Has Mr. Clapperton really seen a Unicorn? If he had met a Unicorn, why hadn't he told anyone? He could've become famous! Why, Why, Why?

Oh, there were so many questions in my mind. I didn't realise when I slept.

I woke up and rubbed my eyes. Then, I remembered last night's events. I tried to forget them but could not.

"I should talk to someone about this," I said to myself while taking a bath.

I was eating my breakfast when I thought that with whom I should talk about this. Grown-ups would be useless because they would not believe me. I should talk to someone who is of my age. Yes! Sam! He would be great. He will believe me.

After finishing my breakfast, I went to Sam's house. He told me to wait for him in the basketball court as he was having his breakfast. I went under that tree and waited for him for some time. After some time, Sam also came there.

"Yes, what were you saying?" He asked.

Then I told him all about the things that happened last night and also about my dream.

After hearing the story, he said, "I don't believe this. But it could be a horse too. And if it was a Unicorn, why hadn't he told anyone?"

"Hey I just remembered," I said, "If people come to know that Unicorns do exist, they would use them for their own good. Same was the case with that flightless bird Dodo, which has now become extinct. There are many such animals that the people trap or kill. One such bird is Kakapo, which was found in New Zealand. Now there are only a few of them left."

Sam was listening with great interest. Then, he said, "Oooh, *now* I understood why he kept Unicorns a secret." This finished the talk.

After that, our friends arrived. We played a Basketball match with them. After the match, we all were very much tired.

Just then, Sam said to me, "Hey, my injury no longer hurts. So can we go to those fields near those woods tomorrow?"

I was about to answer when David, who was our other friend, asked, "Can we all also join you?"

"Okay!" Sam said.

Leo said, "So it is decided. We all will meet tomorrow in front of Sam's house at 10 am."

I nodded and said, "Someone should also bring a mobile phone. We can inform our parents if anything happens."

Sam said, "I'll bring it!"

We all agreed and went to our houses. I told my Uncle and Aunt about this, quickly ate my dinner, went to my room and slept heartily. The next day changed everything!

□

3

The Secret of the Forest

When I woke up, sunlight was pouring in on my bed through the window. I rubbed my eyes and looked at the clock. Oh! 9.30...what???? I looked at the clock again, hoping that I was dreaming. No change in the time. It was decided. We had to go to the fields at 10 am.

"All my friends would be leaving their houses right now," I said to myself while having a bath.

It was 10.15 when I left the farmhouse. I took my bike and went to Sam's house. My friends were waiting there for me with their backpacks.

Sam said, "Hey, at last you arrived. Now only Kevin is left. And look, "He took out a cell phone from his pocket. "Mum let me carry this."

Just as he said the last word, his cell phone rang. He answered and after some time, he kept the phone back in his pocket.

Leo asked, "What happened?"

"Kevin has a fever. So, he will not be able to come. His mother told me just now," Sam said with a sigh.

"Now let us go to the fields without him." I suggested.

We all left the farms. I was cycling at the last. My friends were laughing and talking but I was thinking about the creature which I saw in Mr. Clapperton's garage. Were there really Unicorns in this world? If there were, why hasn't anybody found them yet?

My thoughts were interrupted by Sam who came near my cycle.

"Hey, are you still thinking about that unicorn thing? Forget it. There are no creatures like Unicorns. Let's enjoy now." I saw a sparkle into his green eyes when he said this.

We reached to the fields in about ten minutes. The fields were bright as the sun was slowly coming overhead. We first explored them, then spread a blanket on a clear patch of grass and sat down to play something. Sam took out an empty bottle from his bag and suggested that we should play T.D.S., that is, Task, Dance, Song, with it.

"Hey, yes it's a good idea," David said.

So, we sat down to play. The bottle first pointed towards Leo. He chose to accept a task.

Andy said, "You will have to climb a tree. This is your task."

Everybody agreed to this task. Leo got up to climb a tree but fell every time he tried. Then we continued our game.

The bottle turned towards me next. I also accepted to take a task as I thought that they will give me the same task as was given to Leo and I was very good at it. But I was wrong. They gave me a completely different task.

Sam said after discussing with other friends, "We give you the task to go inside those woods and spend 15 minutes there."

I tried to protest when a thought struck me. If I said no, they will think that I am a coward and they will make fun of me.

So I said, "yes!" under peer pressure and went inside that strange forest.

Dry leaves were scattered on all over the path and were making crunching noises under my feet. I was going deeper into the forest. In the way I saw many plants and trees whose names I didn't remember or didn't know.

The scene looked awfully familiar to me. Then I remembered that all this had happened in that strange dream.

I looked back to make sure that no one was following me. Then I looked in front but nobody was there also.

Just then, I heard distant hoof beats. Then I saw a whitish creature coming towards me. He looked like the same Unicorn who came in my dream but I was not sure.

I ran back, tripped and fell. I picked up a sharp stick and pointed it towards him.

"Do not come near me. I will hit you." That was a foolish thing to say.

The Unicorn halted and spoke, "Do not be scared. I am here just to tell you that we need you. I told that to you in your dream."

"S...So you *are* the one w...who came in m...my dream?" I stammered. I was not sure whether this was a dream or not.

"Yes, you are correct. And all this is not a dream. We all are real and we will not hurt you," he seemed to read my mind.

I started to convince my mind that all this was real. The Unicorn continued, "Parth, we all need you. Please come with me."

"But I cannot. My Uncle will be looking for me," I told him my problem.

"Oh, all that time will be reduced and no one will know that you were missing."

I decided to trust him. I had no other choice left. He told me to sit on his back and we took off.

I asked him all that I wanted to know in the way, "How do you know my name? Is Mr. Clapperton with you? Where are we going? What is your name?"

"Stop, my friend, I can only answer one question at a time. My name is Stan. We are going to Florencia," he replied calmly.

"Florencia, what is it?"

"It is the place where all the Unicorns reside."

I was stunned to hear that there was a place where Unicorns lived. I asked again, "How is this city hidden?"

Florencia has a vast shield on its boundaries. If any human comes near its boundaries, except you and Mr. Clapperton, he will automatically reach to the other side without knowing it."

I asked about Mr. Clapperton, "When I and my friend went into our neighbour, Mr. Clapperton's garage, we found tons of books about Unicorns. So, is he with you?"

"Yes. He learned about us when he was camping in this forest. This happened about 10 years ago. It was the first time when a modern human learned about us and now you also know it."

"So, he is with you!!?" I was astonished.

"Yes, Mr. Clapperton is with us since then and is helping us in a very big problem," he stopped like he did not want me to know what the problem was.

"Helping you in a *very* big problem?" I repeated, "What is it?"

"The Prime Unicorn will tell you about that."

Before I could say anything, Stan said, "We have reached there. In front of you is Florencia."

□

4
Florencia's Problem

At first nothing was visible except trees and plants but then I felt a small jerk and I saw the real Florencia. The sight before my eyes was unbelievable.

There were plants everywhere and even the houses were covered with plants. All the houses were wooden except one tower-like building. It was very wide and had a large terrace. The terrace was half covered and a large group of animals was standing on the remaining part. The city was covered by tall walls on all the sides except the one through which Stan and I had entered.

In the beginning, I had doubts but now I was positive that I was day-dreaming. I pinched myself and it was not a dream. Then I noticed one thing. The houses and streets were empty. Not a single creature was there.

I asked Stan, "Hey, Stan! Where is everybody?"

"They must be up in that tower. The Prime Unicorn was about to call a meeting."

"Oh yes! I forgot to ask who is Prime Unicorn?"

"He is the leader of all of the creatures living in Florencia. We have a ritual in which three of the most good and able Unicorns are chosen by all the people and the Uniball chooses the one who is required to lead Florencia."

"It was done forty years ago. The Unicorn, who is chosen, rules till he is not able to do so. Then the next elections are held. The Prime Unicorn is the most clever and good creature in Florencia. He knows everything and his magic is powerful than all of us as he faces the Uniball." Stan finished.

I asked again, "What is Uniball? By your way of talking about it, the Uniball seems an important thing."

He answered, "Yes, the Uniball is very important but only Prime Unicorn can tell more you about it."

With that answer, our series of questions ended as we reached into the city side. I looked around my surroundings and was amused by them.

There was a small lawn in front of every house but no one could be seen. Only some birds flew towards that tower. We came to a halt in front of that tower.

Stan said, "Parth, now hold on to me tightly as I am going to fly over the top of that tower."

I closed my hands around his neck and his horn glowed. The next moment, we were *flying* and I was both scared and amazed.

At last, we reached on top of the tower. There were Unicorns, animals and even humans on the top. Standing in the middle was an older Unicorn who was different from all of them. He had a light golden horn and his eyes were the most affectionate eyes I had ever seen.

I guessed that he was the Prime Unicorn. When he saw me, his face broke into a smile. Then, he spoke,

"Welcome, my dear friend. We have been waiting for you. Thanks Stan, for bringing Parth here."

Stan bowed his head very low and went backwards into the group of those animals. The Prime Unicorn came near me and said, "All the creatures of Florencia, our savior has arrived. Now, the power of the Uniball will be restored soon and we will have peace all over Florencia."

I was not sure that I heard correctly when he said that I was their savior. Then Prime Unicorn told others to return to their daily chores.

Afterwards, he said, "Dear Parth, we all had been waiting for you. Come on, follow me!"

We went into a room which was situated downstairs. While going down, I asked, "May I ask you a question, Prime Unicorn?"

"Yes, yes, Parth! Queries should always be solved." He replied eagerly.

"Why did you choose *me*? I am only an ordinary kid and I am not from this place. I am from India." I said.

"That was why I chose you. Actually, we didn't choose you. The Uniball did and you don't know how many powers you have. There is another secret, but I will tell you that when you return from this task. Parth, you are unique and special. Just as your Indian god Hanuman had to be reminded of his powers, similarly, you also have to recognise your powers," the Prime Unicorn replied. We started moving downstairs.

I was amused, "How do you know about our Indian mythology?"

"Yes, we know everything about every mythology. This is because the Uniball is a universal power and it has tons of knowledge stored in it. When I became the Prime Unicorn, I had to give myself in to the Uniball. That is why I know all this!" he replied.

We stopped before a golden iron door. The Prime Unicorn inserted his horn in a hole, probably a key hole, and the door opened. His horn was the key of that door. Although there were no candles lit or lamps burning, there was a strange glow in that room.

All the light was coming from a small box kept in the centre of the room. I deduced that this was where that Uniball was kept.

The Prime Unicorn said, "This place is called the Uni-chamber."

"In that meeting, you said that I was your savior. From whom should I save you?" I asked.

He started to explain, "Look, for some time, the Uniball started showing signs that its energy was becoming low. I think that someone is stealing the energy. If the Uniball loses its energy continuously, the earth will die."

"But why will our earth die?"

"Do you know what the first living creatures on earth were?"

"Yes. They were the bacteria and algae." I was not sure why he was asking all this.

"How did they come into existence?" He asked further.

I replied, "Um... because the conditions were right?"

"But what made the conditions correct?" He paused. Then said, "The Uniball."

"When earth was uninhabited, the most powerful alien race, at that time, the Mandators sent a life force called the Uniball to earth. The Uniball started the life process on earth. Now if the Uniball will lose all its energy, the earth will again become deserted as Uniball maintains the natural phenomenon. So, we need you to bring back that stolen power and restore it back into the Uniball." The Prime Unicorn finished.

For me, knowing and experiencing all this was no more than a dream but I had to believe it. I was also thrilled to know that there were aliens living in some part of the universe. I asked again, "You said that the Mandators were the most powerful alien race *at that time*. Who is the most powerful now?"

"That secret is still unknown. The Mandators decreased and went into hiding. Nobody knows where they are now or what happened to them afterwards." He answered calmly. "Now do you have any questions?"

"How did Unicorns evolve?" I asked.

"No one knows that the Uniball, along with making good conditions for the organisms to evolve, also produced an entirely different organism – Stux. This Stux developed and two unusual creatures – the Unicorns and the Centaurs, along with different monsters developed."

I was flabbergasted. There were Centaurs and Monsters too. Then a thought struck me. The Prime Unicorn had not told me who stole the energy of Uniball. So, were they....

"Yes, you are thinking correct. The Centaurs stole the Uniball's energy. So... are you ready for this adventure?"

I thought for some time and said, "But...Um...Can you yourself not do it? I don't know anything about this place and its people. Then how will I fight for you?"

"I am not allowed to leave Uniball and the Uniball wants you to do this work. It's your destiny. Only you will be able to do this work, Parth! Our enemies will not be expecting a human, especially a kid, to fight them. This is a big advantage!"

"Okay. If you say, then I promise that I'll try my best in this quest and I *will* bring back the Uniball's power to you," I answered with determination in my heart.

"Very good, and one more thing, you will tell no one about us. Not even your uncle and aunt."

I asked, "But why should I not tell anyone about this?" I wanted to tell all of this to Sam.

"You yourself figured it out. You humans are very fond of development. If other humans will find about us, they will try to earn money, will try to capture our energy and, ultimately, the Uniball! If this happens, the end of the world is a must. Now if you will go to Mr. Clapperton, he will help you more," the Prime Unicorn finished.

I quickly asked, "Hey, what will I tell my uncle and aunt when I return? Also, while I am in Florencia, they will be looking for me. I will be possibly spending days here. What will happen then?"

"Mr. Clapperton will tell you about it." He led me to that box from which all the light was coming. He opened it and I saw the most beautiful ball of blue light. It appeared to be transparent and had blue smoke inside it. I could spend a whole day watching it.

I spoke without knowing, "How beautiful it is!"

"Yes! The ball of light, it has many mysteries and histories inside it." He suddenly sounded like in a trance. Then he quickly recollected himself and said, "Touch it and you will reach to the place where Stan met you. Go on. I'll be waiting for you."

I touched the Uniball and closed my eyes. It was warm and full of life. A rush of energy flowed through my veins. When I opened my eyes again, I found myself back in that forest. I was very much excited as an adventure awaited me.

□

5
A Helping Hand

I looked at my watch. I had spent only 10 minutes in Florencia. "Hey, it looked like an hour there!" I said to myself.

I ran back to our picnic place. My friends were chatting when I went there. David said, "Hey, don't you remember? You had to stay in the forest for 15 minutes."

I said, "I am not feeling well. So, I am going to my house."

"Should I come with you?" Sam said, carefully looking at me.

"No!" I was surprised by my sudden change of tone. "I'll go on my own. I mean… you should stay here and enjoy."

I took my backpack, took my bicycle and pedaled towards the farms. My plan was to go to Mr. Clapperton's house right now and tell him about this unexpected meeting.

His dark house came into view. As usual, the curtains of the house were closed and some noises could be heard from his garage. I parked my bike into my farm, as it was very close, and went to his house.

I rang the doorbell and waited. After some time, the door opened and he peeked through a narrow opening.

"What do you want?" He asked in a harsh voice.

I leaned closer and told him, "I know about Florencia and that problem. I learned it just now and came to...."

"Quiet! Get in, fast." He cut me short again.

I went in. The whole house was covered with shelves full of books. In a corner, a computer was kept. A picture of a unicorn and a big article was written on its monitor.

Mr. Clapperton said, "So, have you met the Prime Unicorn?" His tone had changed and it was slightly soft now.

I answered, "Yes, he told me to go to your house so that you could help me."

"Yes, yes! I was waiting for the person whom the Prime Unicorn had chosen. But I had expected someone big. Anyways, now let me find that map."

He began searching through the drawers and at last inside a small drawer, a very old and yellow piece of paper was found.

I looked at the paper but nothing was written on it. How could the blank thing show me my way? Then Mr. Clapperton again took out a strange thing. It was hollow and triangular from the front and flat from the behind. There was a long chain attached to its one side so that it could be worn around the neck.

He took the thing and placed it in the middle of that paper. As he started to rotate it, golden lines began forming on the piece of paper and it began expanding. I was very much amused.

He explained, "This is the map and this," he held out the strange thing, "is the Madges. It is the key of this map. Without it, no one will be able to read this map. These madges can also save you but only once. After it has saved you, you should immediately take it off and throw it as it burns after a heavy strike on it," he locked the map and I kept it in my pocket.

"And," he continued, "you will also face many difficulties on this journey but the most fierce one lies at the end. You will also face many monstrous beasts in the way. For that, I could give you one thing."

I was very much excited. I thought of some shiny sword but when he took out the thing from a bookshelf, I felt like a dozen stones falling on my head. It was a book. Okay, I liked books, but a sword or a weapon would have helped more on this journey!

He said, "I know you expected some shiny weapon, but that was a thing of the past. Today, it is the time of knowledge. I can also give you a helper."

He took out an old, black leather jacket. This is a gift from the Prime Unicorn to whoever is the savior of Florencia. Any questions that you want to ask?"

I told him, "While I am gone, my uncle and aunt will be worried about me. What about their worries?"

"I have invented a machine which could convert days into minutes. That will help you," he said.

"When do I start the journey?"

"You will start the journey now!"

"Now... really, you must be joking! I have no preparations for this!"

"Then go home and make the preparations for your journey. You will start now. It will be good because the sooner you start the journey, the sooner you return."

I started to leave when Mr. Clapperton said a sentence which filled courage in me.

I went back to my farmhouse, thinking about that line. I had to believe in myself. Mr. Clapperton had said, "Nothing is difficult in the world if you have the will and determination in your heart to reach or obtain it because where there is a will, there is always a way."

□

6
Preparations for the Journey

I entered into my room. Nobody had seen me when I arrived into the farmhouse. Aunt Kshama was in the kitchen and Uncle Dhairya must have gone to the city. The jacket, the map and that book were on my table. I was searching for things that could be useful. I had taken a bottle full of water, 2-3 coins (I didn't know of what use they would be!) and a small torch. I had put the coins in a pocket of the jacket.

I picked up that book. It had a very old binding and nothing was written on its brown cover. I opened the book. Its title was written in Latin-'In Eu Monstra'. The book was a translated version. In English it was called-'The Encyclopedia of Monsters'. When I flipped the other pages, I came to know that the book had two books in one. The other book was called – 'Et Fines Ejus Florencia' or 'Florencia and its Boundaries'.

I stuffed the book along with other things in my bag. I had also taken a spare pair of jeans and a blue t-shirt.

Afterwards I had a shower and wore my long, tight jeans and a half, blue shirt with checks on it. I, then, wore that black, leather jacket which Mr. Clapperton had given to me. I hanged the backpack onto my shoulders and went downstairs.

When Aunt Miranda saw me, she asked, "Parth, where are you going with such heroic appearance?"

I lied, "Me and my friends are going to the countryside."

"But why are you wearing a jacket in summer?"

"I...I found it in the closet," I lied again.

"Yes, but why are you wearing it?" she asked puzzled.

"I'm wearing it... just for style." I could not think of a better answer. I started to leave when aunt said, "Have you got anything to eat?"

"Um...no, I don't have anything," I hadn't even thought of it.

She gave me tiffin in which five muffins and a banana were packed. I kept it in my bag and left the farmhouse. I took my bike and went towards the direction of the woods.

In the way, Sam met me. "I was just coming to your house." He said, "How are you now? And where are you going?"

I just answered, "I can't tell you now. I'm in a hurry."

He was watching me as if he was suspicious. I pedaled fast and reached to the place where Stan had met me.

"Where should I go now?" I muttered. Suddenly, with a screeching noise, an arrow was encrusted on a tree bark somehow, pointing to where I should go. I went in that direction.

I reached to the place where that shield was formed. I could see it. It had a whitish blue color. I doubted whether I could go in or not. But, I was sucked in when I put my index finger into that shield. My bike was left outside. I ran straight towards the high tower. I stopped in front of the tower.

"How will I reach to the top?" I wondered.

A doorway appeared in front of me and I went in. I crossed the Uni-chamber and went to the top. The Prime Unicorn was standing opposite the stairway, looking towards the city. When he heard me coming, he came towards me.

"I saw you coming. Have you met Mr. Clapperton, Parth?" he asked calmly.

"Yes, and he also gave me a map, a book and this jacket but I don't know how will I use these things!" I told him my worry.

"You will have to figure that out yourself. Just believe in yourself and everything will become clear." He said.

"Okay, I will do that!" I felt disheartened. "So, can I start my journey?" I was excited about that.

"Stay calm, my friend, and you look good in this jacket," he complimented.

"Thanks!" I again started feeling good.

He started walking towards a golden door which I had first ignored. "Let us discuss what you have to do and where you should go," I followed him.

The room was fully dark. The Prime Unicorn's horn lighted up the room. It was filled with a yellow and warm light. We went to a long table. I took out the map from my pocket and placed it on the table. Then, I took out the madges which I had worn around my neck. I unlocked the map and put the madges back inside my shirt.

In one corner of the map was the usual direction-telling sign. For the first time, I saw the full map. Florencia was so big!

The city was in the east. The western side was full of forests. In the south was a village and in the south-east, a big river was separating the forests and the village. There was a long row of volcanoes in the north. The river was called 'Kandge' and it was flowing first towards the east, then to the north and then again to the east. The river separated Florencia into two parts – the mountains and the forests in the north and west and the city and the village in the south.

The volcanoes were called 'Paradise of hell'. The name does look weird but, again, it's a name. The village was not far from the city. Its name was 'Village of Workers'.

The Prime Unicorn said, "Your destination is beyond the Paradise of hell. There is a dark forest that does not come in the reign of Florencia for it is the residence of all the fierce creatures including trolls, giants, and all the weird creatures you can imagine. There is the fortress of centaurs too. You should go in it and find the stolen energy. You should bring it back safely."

I again took out the madges and without locking the map, kept it in my pocket.

"You should first go to the Village of Workers. There you will find a companion. He or *she* will help you in your journey. You should take him with you and then cross the river. Then, you should walk parallel to the river in the direction of the volcanoes as there is an entrance to the mountains."

"You will face many difficulties but you should face them bravely. Compared to the danger you will be fighting with, in the last, these difficulties are nothing."

I gulped. Was he indirectly telling me that I could die on this mission?

"Now, Parth," he said, his horn glowing suddenly, "Your journey begins!"

As he finished the last word, a doorway appeared towards my right. It was covered with a silver mist. I stepped through it and my adventure began. □

7
The Journey Begins

I stepped on dry grass. This place looked like a plain ground. I looked behind. There was the vast wall. From a distance, it looked fine but on a closer look, it was so high that I needed to tilt my head at full 90 degrees. I took out the map from my pocket and shot a quick glance at it before locking it. I had to go towards my south.

I searched my jacket's pocket to see if it had anything. I felt something solid into my fingers. When I took it out, I was overjoyed. It was a compass! I studied it and started walking towards south. I was feeling awful walking blankly. I wanted to reach that village as fast as I could, so I started to run.

Actually, it was a foolish act because, from nowhere, three terrible dogs came running towards me. Their mouths were horrifically large and they were barking at me madly.

I ran with my full force. I was screaming, "Help, help." It was again an imbecile action as there was no one in that place for miles. I also had to keep positioning my backpack because it kept sliding off my shoulder.

Then, I saw a tree which, I thought, I could climb to escape those dogs. When I reached near the tree,

I saw that it was unusually tilted to one side, which acted as a platform for me to climb. I climbed to the highest branch panting and short of breath. When I looked down, the dogs were nowhere to be seen.

But I took a precaution and stayed on that branch for thirty minutes more. During that time, I studied the compass and looked out for those dogs. I also ate one of the muffins that Aunt Kshama had given to me.

After drinking some water, I climbed down and started again. I chose to walk rather than run as I was afraid that I might attract some other monster. I was getting bored. So, I took out that book which Mr. Clapperton had said will help me. I opened the index. The names of different monsters were arranged alphabetically. I recognised some of them like centaurs, unicorns, griffins, Minotaur, giants, trolls, etc.

Then, I flipped a bundle of pages and there it was, the same beast that was chasing me. It was called a Hellhound. It hated loud voices and people running. Actually, the hellhounds were descendants of the great hound of hell called Cerberus, who guards doors of hell. All this was written in the description of it. Hellhounds kill anyone unknown who comes near it. I gulped. I had just escaped death.

I looked in front. A small hut was standing two meters away. I kept the book back in my bag. I was suspicious at first, but after observing it fully from outside, I went inside. Tables of sweets were kept in it. I rushed towards them without thinking twice. When I touched the first table, my hand went right through it.

Then, I realised that all this was a trap. I turned for the exit but it was gone! I turned back towards the table but it had disappeared too. In its place was a pile of skeletons which almost freaked me out. I quickly tried to think something but my mind was not with me. I was really scared.

I put my hands into the pockets of my jacket. A handful of something round came in my hands. I took one out. It was a marble. What kind of a jacket was this? – I thought. I threw the marble on that pile of bones. The moment it touched the land, it blasted. I was shaken from head to toe.

Then a plan came crashing in my mind. It was insane. It was dangerous. But it was my last hope. I filled both my hands with those blasting marbles and threw them on one side of that hut. I had closed my ears but the blast almost pierced my eardrums. I was not able to hear a sound for very long. At last, I opened my eyes and looked towards the big hole that I had made.

But the hole was becoming shorter. It looked as if the hut was healing itself. I ran outside with full speed and fell on the ground. When I looked back at that hut, it had healed itself and was fading away. I got up to my feet and hung the backpack on my shoulders. I noticed that it was night time and the only light was coming from the moon. When I had entered the hut, it was afternoon. It seemed as if five minutes in there were five hours outside.

I started to walk again. I walked for about two hours. After that, I got exhausted and sat down. I gathered some twigs to light a fire and searched for a lighter. As usual, I found it in one of the pockets of my jacket. I had learned the secret of this jacket. Whenever I wanted some help, a related object appeared in this jacket's pockets. First, I needed a compass, it appeared in a pocket. Then I needed to get out of that hut and those marbles appeared. And now this lighter! Now I understood why Mr. Clapperton had called this jacket 'a helper'.

I lied down, and was watching the stars. I had never believed that these fairytale creatures existed. Now, I was on a quest to find and bring the power of a ball called the Uniball from centaurs to the unicorns and I was going to face many monsters. All this was impossible but, yet, it *was* real. Yes, I had dreamt of going on an extraordinary adventure but dreaming is very different from really being on an unusual adventure.

I was missing my parents and the real world. Although this place was good, but I lived outside it. I had to go very far and I was still thinking about my decision. I knew that there was no backing off. I had accepted this quest. I had to finish it myself.

There was no sleep in my eyes. So, I started to count the stars. I soon got bored. At last, sleep closed my eyes. I needed to get rest because I had a very long way to go. I also had to find that person who would become my companion.

□

8
Selira

I woke up in a comfortable and cozy bed. At first, I thought that I was in my room in India. Then, after some time, I remembered that I was in Florencia on a quest. I jumped from the bed and asked myself, “Where am I?” I looked around. This place looked like a well-built house.

“You’re in the Village of the Workers!” someone said from behind me.

I turned back and saw a thin, old man sitting on a chair. I asked him, “Where is my bag?”

I thought it sounded rude. So, I quickly asked, “Sorry for my tone but can you tell me how I came here?”

He said, “Your bag is in that cupboard over there.” He pointed to a small cupboard in a corner.

While I went there and took out my backpack, he said, “We were hunting at night. We found you sleeping in a very dangerous place. So, we carried you here. You were in a deep sleep. So, we thought it best not to wake you up.”

I was surprised to know that I slept so heavily, but was also happy that I reached this village so easily. I asked for the permission to leave, “Um... I have to go now. I...came here to take someone with me.”

"But where are you going?" he asked.

I thought for some time that should I tell him about the purpose of my journey.

He said, "Okay, I understand that it is a secret. Well, now you may go," he sighed.

'I came out of that house and started to walk towards my left. What a pleasant old man!' I thought.

All the people were working in this village. Some were making pots and wooden things. Some were sewing dresses. There were also candy shops and toy shops.

Then my eyes fell on a shop which was unexpected in Florencia. It was *multimedia* shop. I never thought that these people could even know what a cell phone is. But here was a full shop of these items!

I saw some children playing but none was of my age. Then I went to that multimedia store. I wanted to know if they had smartphones too.

I asked the shopkeeper, "Do you have any smartphones?"

He nodded. He was reading a book.

I asked again, "What is the cost of a smartphone?"

He said without raising his face, "Five Stellarum!"

I was not sure that I heard correct, "What? What is a stellarum?"

Now he raised his face, "You are not from Florencia. Am I right?"

I was not prepared for such question. I tried to think of what answer I should give.

He said, "Never mind. Stellarum is the currency of Florencia."

"Oh." I had not thought of it. I put my hand in my pocket to give him the coins, hoping that he would accept them. When I inserted my hand in my pocket, something pointy came in my hand. When I took it out, I understood that those coins had been converted into stars, the currency of Florencia.

Those things had the shape of stars. There was a picture of Uniball on one side of that star. The other side had a picture of that tower in which the Uniball was kept.

I gave those stars to the shopkeeper. He took them and gave me a real smartphone. It was the best phone I had ever seen in my life. It had a curved screen with colour that changed according to our mood. The android version was 9.03 Munch. I don't know why they always keep the name of a chocolate! All that time, the shopkeeper was watching me continuously. I felt a little uncomfortable.

I asked him, "Why is this phone so inexpensive?"

He answered, "We people do not use any electronic things much. These smartphones are just to call our relatives who live in the city." I kept the phone in the pocket of my jacket which had a zip. Then, I turned to go back.

I went out of that shop. I wanted to ask someone about a place where I might find warriors. I asked a potter, "Do you know where I can find some good warriors?"

"They may be in the Gross Arena, but why do you want to go there? Big fights are held there. That is not a place for kids," he said.

"No I was just asking." I didn't convey that I was about to go there. I searched on the smartphone's GPS about Gross Arena and the way was clear. But to confirm,. I asked that potter, "If anyone wants to go there…?"

"Just take this straight path and it will be in front of you," he said and again got engaged in his work. This meant that the GPS was working correctly.

"Thank you!" I said and went on that way. I walked for about an hour. After that, I could see a filthy building in front of me. It was the Gross Arena.

I entered into it. A faint odour caught my breath. It smelled like a rotten fish. As I walked further, the odour kept becoming stronger. Now I understood why this arena was called gross.

There were about two hundred people sitting there but they did not seem to mind the smell. Two gladiators were fighting there. One was much shorter than the other; he was probably of my height but with that big man, he looked like a dwarf. They were wearing a suit of armour.

Both the gladiators were fighting fiercely. I was thinking how this dwarf will fight the big man. He was fighting very quickly and his defense was also very fast. He dodged most of the strikes and smashed the big man's back with the hilt of his sword.

Suddenly, the dwarf's opponent kicked him in the stomach and he fell down. The big man raised his sword to attack him.

'This is the end of him'. I thought.

But he did a sudden back-flip on the ground and threw some sand in the eyes of the man. The whole crowd was yelling the name of that big man. He was called Smacker.

So, Smacker was startled with sand in his eyes. Then that dwarf kicked him in the shins and he fell on his knees. I thought that he was going to kill Smacker but he grabbed the big man's helmet and threw it on the ground. Smacker's face was not visible clearly. Suddenly, he tried to hit the dwarf with his sword but the dwarf was quick. He swiftly defended himself with his sword and then kicked the big man in the stomach. Smacker was already on the ground and after the kick, he lost hold of his sword and leaned more. His face came forward. The dwarf cought the big man's sword and hit him forcefully on the nose with his knee.

The next moment, Smacker was completely lying on the ground, holding his nose. The dwarf pointed both the swords on his neck and said, "You are defeated Smacker! Go and tell everyone that a *girl* has defeated you."

A girl??? I was astonished. Now I understood that there was a girl in that suit of armour. I knew that I had to take her with me. My instincts were telling me that she could help me. The girl had gone out of the arena by the back door. I ran to catch up with her.

She had taken off her helmet and was combing her long black hair with her hand. She had a very slight dark complexion.

I shouted, "Hey, who are you and what are you doing here?" That absolutely sounded rude but I had to stop her.

She turned towards me. She had a cute face and was about my age. Her height was a little shorter than me, perhaps an inch or two. She had brown eyes and a short nose. She looked offended by my question as she gave me a penning stare.

"I just wanted to say that you are a great fighter.

I was told that this is no place for kids, but... you defeated a big warrior! That's totally awesome.

"If it is not a place for kids, then what are you doing here?" she asked. Her voice was slightly high-pitched but was good.

"Oh, I... just came here to watch you fighting!" I answered sarcastically.

"Really, you are very smart!!" And we both started laughing.

"Look I am new here, so... won't you ask me for coffee?"

"It seems that now I should take you to a cafe." After some talking, I got to know that she already knew me as it was her grandfather who brought me to this village at night.

Then, I told her my full story of coming to Florencia and about that quest. After hearing all that, she said, "From my side, I'm in. But..."

"What?" I was afraid that she would tell me that her grandpa will not agree.

"I have to ask my grandfather. I know that he would let me go. I always wanted to go on a quest like this!" she beamed with joy.

'Now I could only hope that her grandfather would agree. I would also tell her grandfather that Prime Unicorn had told me to take her with me,' I thought.

"Hey, I forgot!" I asked, "What's your name?"

"First tell me what *your* name is?" she asked, giving me a dazzling smile.

"My name is Parth," I said.

"Hi Parth, my name is Selira, Selira Lester."

□

9
The Monstrous River

We had crossed the village and were moving towards the river Kandge. I had spent a day in the Village of Workers.

After the coffee, Selira and I had gone to her grandfather. We asked for the permission of the old man whose name was Lester Ronald. I had to tell him everything about my journey and after thirty minutes of convincing him by Selira, we got his permission to go on. Selira had shown me the full village in one day. Everyone seemed to know her. She had also taken a small bag with packed food for five-six days.

I was always shy before girls and never talked to them without any purpose. Now I had to *go* on a full journey with a girl whom I didn't know. I was walking ahead of Selira. She was thinking something. We both were quiet. Selira also had two swords, a long rope and a dagger with her.

I took out the map. I still had that Madges around my neck. When I took it out, she said, "Hey, what is that?"

"It's a map which opens with this key, called the Madges," I said, holding out that locket. I unlocked the map.

"It's awesome!" Selira said as she saw the map expanding and lines forming on it.

We were going in the right direction. Selira asked, "Do you know sword fighting?"

"Um…no, But from where did you learn all those smart moves?" I said.

"I made all the moves myself," she explained further, "You see, sometimes when I am fighting or practising, fight moves eventually come in my mind. Like that back flip move in the arena? It was a quick thought."

I was astounded. Really, Selira could help me on this mission. Suddenly, she said, "I can train you! I will teach you some of my favorite moves, if you want," she added. I didn't know what to reply. So, I stayed silent.

Selira had changed her clothes. She was wearing a blue t-shirt and a green skirt. Beneath it, she was wearing sky-blue jeans. She still had her weapons. There was a dagger and a sword on either sides of her waist.

"Why are you carrying so many weapons?"

"They can be used anytime, anywhere and on this mission, we will need them frequently," she answered.

I was still thinking that whether she could teach me or not, when Selira pointed to our front and said, "There is the river Kandge!"

From her, I remembered Sam. What would he be doing now? – I wondered – What if I had also taken him with me. I would have someone to talk to. Okay, Selira was with me but she was a girl, and there are some things that remain between boys.

The river was before us and it was evening. So, we decided to spend the night on the riverbank. We lit a small fire.

I asked her a question to break the silence, "So, Selira! Why is your surname 'Lester'?"

She answered cheerfully, "Actually my great-great grandfather was an orphan. He didn't have any surname. After he got married and had a son and that son had a son, that is my great-great grandfather's grandson, that grandson kept his grandfather's name as his surname. So, we have this tradition and my surname is the name of my grandfather," she smiled.

I smiled back and again asked, "Okay. And where are your parents?"

I had asked the wrong question as she suddenly became very sad. "We were separated, I mean..." she paused, and then sighed.

"I will tell you the whole story. My father was a blacksmith. He made weapons for the army of Florencia. So, he took me and my mother to the city often. I was five years old then. One night, we were coming back when I felt hungry and started to cry. They saw a small hut and told me to stay out and wait. They went inside and the door vanished. They never came back. My grandfather found me at daytime."

We became silent then. After some time, I heard a small sob from Selira. I tried to comfort her, "Don't cry, Selira. Please don't cry."

"It was en... entirely my fault. I s...should not h... have cried," she said between sobs.

"It was not your fault. Anyone could become hungry at any time. And you were just a child," I said.

She cried for a few minutes and then slept peacefully. After a while, I too felt my eyes heavy and went to sleep.

I was running. Someone was behind me. It looked like it was night time. I was completely surrounded by trees with very big roots growing out of the earth. Suddenly I stumbled on a root and fell down. A dark shadow came over me and started strangling me.

I woke with a start. There were weeds all around me. Wait, *weeds*?!! What were *they* doing here?

I called Selira, "Selira. Where are you? We are trapped. Help me!"

"I am down at the bottom but where are you?" her voice came at last.

"I am here. Down. Beneath these weeds! Please free me," I said after gathering some strength. It looked as if those weeds were sucking all my strength.

Out of the corner of my eye, I saw Selira's dagger fallen besides me. I grabbed it and started to cut the weeds. Then, I also freed Selira and we climbed on a strong tree. After getting on a large branch, we saw that those weeds sucked everything that came beneath them.

I thought – I had been awake for about an hour. So, why didn't they come then?

But then I saw that the place where we had lit our fire was not covered by the weeds. I understood that those weeds were afraid of every light.

I told Selira that these were monstrous weeds and they killed anyone who went near them. They came out only at night as the light could destroy them. Selira was amazed. She asked, "How do you know all these things? Aren't you new here?"

"Yes, I am new here but I read it in a book," I took out that book which Mr. Clapperton had given to me. Selira looked at it for some time and then gave it to me. I kept it back in my backpack. We waited till sunrise and then jumped down from the tree.

I continued, "We cannot stay in the river or in the riverbank. We have to stop every night."

"Yes, so we will walk all day and at night, we'll climb on trees, if you agree," she suggested.

Her plan was good but we would be very late. All the people would be waiting for us, but we had no choice. So we agreed on that plan.

We had to go there faster or else the Centaurs could use the Uniball's power to do bad things. The future of whole Florencia depended on us.

□

10
The Power of a...Pen!!?

At last, we gave up the idea of travelling by the river as it would take weeks to reach to our destination, the Paradise of Hell. We had decided to remain close to the riverbank. For four nights, we climbed onto any strong tree and below us, the weeds destroyed everything.

I had hung my bag on a branch and then looked at my watch. I had spent seven days in Florencia. The day was Friday and it was 4:57 in the morning.

It was impossible to sleep in such noises but somehow Selira was snoring. I was wondering why those hellhounds had not come here. A possibility was that the weeds had scared those dogs and they never came near the banks of Kandge. But we should be alert in this strange place, – I thought.

I had almost forgotten the compass which I had found in my pocket as Selira's sense of direction was very good. I took it out and looked at it. A small button was attached to its bottom.

I pressed it. Nothing happened. I pressed the button again. After pressing it for the third time when nothing happened, I kept it back in my pocket. Sun was about to rise and some light was already lighting the sky. It looked as if someone had switched on the lights of a big room. The difference was that the room was our earth and the light source was the sun.

I called out to Selira. She was sleeping on the tree just opposite to the tree on which I was sleeping. The weeds had gone back into the river.

Selira was not sleeping. She was trying to write something on her dagger with a sharp stone.

She looked towards my tree and said, "Hey Parth. Good morning! Um...but where are you?"

"I'm right here."

"But I can't see you!" She looked all around her.

"Are you playing a pra...?" Suddenly, a thought struck me. I pressed the button on that compass again.

"Whoa! How did you do *that*?" she seemed surprised.

"What did I do?"

"You just appeared out of nowhere. Do you know how to get *invisible*?"

"No, no, no! I just pressed this button and got invisible," I showed her how to do it.

She seemed amazed. "Wow! That was cool!" Then she went back to her work.

I jumped down and asked Selira, "What are you doing up there? Come on, we have to go."

She said, "Please wait for just one second. It's almost done."

After five minutes, she threw the stone and came down. Then she gave me her dagger.

"This is my gift to you, my friend!" she said.

"It's yours. How can I take it?"

"First read what is written on it," she said with a mysterious smile.

I read what was written on the dagger – Parth. I was awe-struck. I was able to say only one thing, "Thanks!"

"Oh, please don't mention that thanks. I hate it among friends. Hey, take this belt too. It will help you to place that dagger on your waist," she gave me a brown belt.

Selira was so good. She had a pure heart.

"You are my real friend!" I said.

She laughed, "Don't make this situation emotional. Come, we have a long way to go."

I tied the belt round my waist. After washing our faces in the cold water of Kandge, we started to walk. I asked Selira, "When did you write all that on this dagger? You were sleeping and I could hear your soft snores."

"Those snores were just to tell you that I was sleeping," she said in a muffled tone as she was eating an apple which she had plucked from a tree.

Suddenly, I heard a loud roar. I looked at Selira. She had already taken out her sword. I took out my dagger.

Another roar, this time closer, was followed by a giant monster. It looked like a big lion with large wings at either side. It was breathing out fire and a python was growing out of the place where its tail was supposed to be.

He jumped on us. Selira threw her apple on that beast and we ran fast. At one point, we split up and the monster went after Selira. It was slow, probably because of its size.

The monster had cornered Selira and was roaring horribly. All this time, I was just standing and looking at whatever was going on. I looked at my dagger. It was definitely not sufficient for the 'Ligon' – as I had read in that book. Then, I picked up a big stone and threw it on the Ligon. It accurately stricked the back side of the head of that beast.

It turned towards me and was about to jump when Selira managed to land a heavy strike on the leg of that monster. Surprisingly, a loud 'CLANG' was produced and the sword fell down from her hands. She just said a long "Ouch!!"

The beast turned back. Selira started running again. She was screaming something but I was not able to hear it because of the Ligon's continuous roars.

Selira had screamed, "Do something! It is made of metal!!"

I again followed them with full speed. On reaching close to the monster, I threw my dagger at it. I expected the dagger to be effective from a shorter distance but the blade simply bounced off the Ligon's back.

I had forgotten the python-tail of that monster but the tail saw me. The three of us – Selira, the Ligon and me, we were running very close to each other. So, the python took advantage of the distance and curled around my wrist. It somehow became longer. I was horrified and screamed. At that precise moment, I stepped on a stone and the stone gave way. My ankle turned and pain shot up my leg.

I was about to fall when the python tightened and with great force, threw me into the river (we were very close to the river). I went underwater with my ankle burning with pain. Thankfully, I knew how to swim underwater but there was no time to celebrate this thing. I looked down. The river was not very deep and the weeds looked pretty now on the riverbed.

Just then, I saw a glimmer near those weeds. A strong urge to go near it brought me closer to the source and on closer observation, I saw that the glimmer was from a crystal which was attached on the top of a pen. I grabbed it and swiftly swam back to the surface. Selira had climbed on a tree and was jumping from one branch to the next. The Ligon was still roaring deafeningly.

Suddenly, the pen got attracted towards the monster, with a great jerk and me holding it tightly. I had to move a few steps forward. A flash of blue light was produced and it was finished!

The roaring had stopped and that Ligon was lying on the ground with a smoky hole in its stomach.

Selira yelled, "*HOW* did you kill it?"

"I...I don't know. This pen just got attracted towards the monster. That flash of light threw the monster and killed it." I said, showing her that pen.

She ran towards me and for the next two hours, she kept looking at the pen and its crystal. I was wet, so I changed my clothes with the spare pair which I had brought. After the drying up of the wet clothes, we continued the journey with a new power.

□

11
The Paradise of Hell

I had forgotten the pain in my ankle but after some time, the pain returned and we had to stop. Selira had a traditional method to cure the wound. Her grandfather had taught her that. She applied some dry soil onto the bruise and covered it with a big leaf. I wanted to tell her that I was fine and we should start going but she said, "No, you will rest here and we will go tomorrow."

I suddenly remembered, "Hey, Selira! Do you remember you asked me that if you could teach me all those fighting moves?"

"Yeah, yeah, so.... What is your answer?" she asked eagerly.

"I...um...My answer is... Yes, I want to learn some fighting skills from you," I said as if I was saying something in a reality show.

Selira jumped up and took out her sword. She did many artful moves with it.

"Come on, let's start now." But then she said nothing and sat down.

"What happened? Aren't we going to start the training now?" I asked.

"But... your ankle is..."

"Oh, it's nothing! I had even forgotten it. Let's start now," I protested.

"As you wish, but you must take care of your foot. Now... first, you should always hold your sword very tightly," Selira said, giving me the other sword which she was carrying. So, we started with the first lesson.

Our swords clashed. Selira's strike was so forceful that my sword fell from my hands.

"Ow! What was the need to strike so hard?" I said angrily.

"Because this is how your enemy will attack you."

"Am I your enemy?" I said picking up the sword.

"You need to be focussed. Your attacker will try to hurt you and your aim is to hurt him. Now copy my moves. Raise your sword like this and..." she started to teach me.

When we stopped our 'training session', it was night time. I was very much tired and hungry. We ate some fruits and then slept heartily.

Selira was already awakened the next day as usual. In our whole journey, she was the one who got up very early.

When I woke up, she said, "Good morning, sleeping beauty!"

"Good...morning!" I said yawning.

"Hey, Parth, can you give me your map? I need to study it," Selira said.

"Yes... just one... minute!" I yawned again and took out the map. I unlocked it and gave it to Selira. She spread it on the ground and after some time, gave it back to me.

"We are not far from the mountains. They are just fifty meters ahead."

I looked above the trees in our front. "But there is no sign of any volcano."

"Obviously, silly boy, those volcanoes are magical. If we do not cross the volcanoes in five hours, the mountains will trap us in them and we'll fade away," Selira added, "As I heard from my grandfather."

"So, we've got five hours after we enter the mountains?"

"Yeah, we need to get out as fast as we can!"

Selira was right. After thirty minutes, we crossed the river by making a small raft and were in front of a large door. Still no volcanoes were visible behind those doors.

I said unconfidently, "Okay, let's go in. Five hours are very long."

We took a long sigh and entered inside. With that, I also started the stopwatch in my watch. The place was horrible! It surely looked like the paradise of hell. Two pillars were standing on either sides of the gate.

The shapes of the volcanoes were very unusual. Some of the volcanoes were round, square, rectangle and triangle. Some were tall, some were short. They all had smoke coming out of them.

The volcanoes were arranged in two rows, one behind the other. Their colour was incredibly red and the plants which were growing on them were the killer plants. They were the extra large versions of the pitcher plants, Venus Fly Trap, etc.

"We need to run fast!" I said.

"Okay, but first let us look around!"

"We've not got much time and our goal is to find and bring back Uniball's stolen power."

"Yes, okay, let us cross these volcanoes," Selira said dishearteningly.

The only shortest way to cross those volcanoes was to go from in between the two rows of the volcanoes. But, there was a large Venus Fly Trap closing every path. We tried to cut them with our swords but it was as if an invisible shield was protecting them.

So, we had to take the much longer route which was to climb the volcano and go back down the other way. We chose a volcano which had the shape of a triangle and behind it, a square-shaped volcano was standing.

When we reached on top of that tall volcano, we had to be careful as there was a lot of smoke and we were crawling on the brink of its vent. Three hours had passed and we still had that square-shaped volcano to climb.

I called out to Selira, "Hey Selira! Do you have anything that could help us climb this volcano?"

As the previous volcano was triangular, so it was comparatively easy to climb it but this was completely vertical. Suddenly I had an idea. I asked Selira for her rope and her sword. Then I tied one end of the rope to the sword and threw it upwards. I went up and probably got stuck in the vent.

"Now, you can climb it and go up faster," I said to Selira.

"No, you go first. I will wait here and don't argue!" She ordered when I opened my mouth to protest, and I had to follow.

I climbed the volcano in thirty minutes. The top of the volcano was completely flat and there was a small vent in the centre. Selira's sword was stuck in it. I reached up and saw all this. I wondered – How can I throw a sword so accurately?

I looked towards Selira and said, "Come up fast. We've got only one hour and thirty minutes."

"Yes, I'm com... aaah!" She had slipped and went down some distance.

I cried out, "Selira...! Are you alright?"

After some time, her voice came from below, "Yes, yes! I am fine. You carry on your downwards journey."

"No, I will wait here for you!"

"Oh, why are all the boys so stubborn?" she asked.

"We are stubborn because you girls never listen to us!" I answered.

Selira started laughing and her laughter was the one which everyone would want to hear. She came up in half-an-hour and we got down in quarter hour as Selira had a strain in her leg.

So, we still had fifteen minutes. In five minutes, we reached in front of the same kind of gates through which we had entered. Suddenly, the door started to close. I looked at the stopwatch. We still had nine minutes and twenty-three seconds. The place was cheating.

Selira said, "Parth, you run! I will look after myself. You are the one who is chosen. Go, it's an order!" she said angrily when I kept standing there.

I ran outside. My legs were longing to return. The gates were closing. I just got out when the doors had closed fully. I looked back. Selira was fading away with the volcanoes. Then, the whole volcanoes faded away and only the doors could be seen. Selira had gone, forever.

□

12

The Dark Forest

It was because of Selira that I was here. She was always with me and now she was gone. What was I to do now? I kneeled down and held my face in my hands. Long, warm streaks of tears came out of my eyes and fell on the ground.

Suddenly, a familiar voice called from behind me, "Parth, I am here!"

I looked back. Selira was standing there. I was so happy that I ran towards her and hugged her tightly. She fell back a few steps. She said, "Whoa! Don't make it dramatic!" I released her quickly. I felt my cheeks becoming red.

I said, "H...how did you escape? You were left there just now!"

"Actually, I forgot to tell you one thing. We can only be trapped inside if we have no physical or very strong mental connection to the outer world."

"But what connected you to the outer world?"

"Do you remember that dagger which I gave you? That was the thing which connected me."

"Thank god, you are with me. I would have been lost in this forest without you," I let out a sigh.

"Why? Am I the forest god?" Selira said. "And... you were also crying," she teased me.

"Okay, okay! Now let us move fast. We are very close to our destination," I said quickly. I was actually very glad that I was not alone on this journey.

After a day's rest, we started again. We had entered into the dark forest. I had read about it in that book which Mr. Clapperton had given to me. The article which I had read was:

The Dark Forest

The boundaries of Florencia are mostly an annex to the outer world. But, the only part which is not connected to the outer world is the beginning of the dark forest. The dark forest has all the hideous monsters and beasts. The dark forest ends on the beginning of the fortress of the centaurs. The centaurs reside in a fortress. When the centaurs were the friends of the unicorns, they lived in a big castle. The dark forest was also under the reign of Florencia. Then, there was some major dispute and the centaurs decided to separate from Florencia.

For years, the centaurs attacked us but they were defeated every time. In the last battle, their leader said, "We are going now, but we will return and will destroy you with your own force."

Then the centaurs established The Paradise of Hell (volcanoes) so that they would be safe from any intruders. They had also fixed certain traps in Florencia in which people get trapped and they reach to Centauria (city of centaurs). They do this because they need more people to help them in their mysterious work which they had been doing since the last battle they fought with Florencia.

There are a number of monsters in the dark forest like Minotaurs, Hellhounds, and Ligons. There are other monsters too that you will find in the Encyclopedia of Monsters. This dark forest is covered with a white mist which carries on the smell of any human travelling there to some monster and the monster kills that person.

This book advises you not to go in that forest.

I gulped when I read the last line. The forest was really covered in a mysterious mist. At first, we faced no problems but after going further on, we faced such monsters that I still have goose-bumps when I think about them.

We found the monster after one day. The first monster was called '*Trosun*'. He was actually a Minotaur.[4] We met him when he was sleeping. We needed to move very slowly and without any noise, so that the beast would not get up. Suddenly, I walked on a pile of branches, collected probably to light a fire. The branches broke with enough noise to wake the monster.

The Trosun sat upright and looked around. Selira and I froze. The beast spotted me.

He roared with his bull-head, "How dare you break my branches! I will kill you."

He had still not spotted Selira. I ran screaming, "Selira, do something fast. He is going to kill me!"

---

4. Minotaur: A Greek monster with the head of a bull and rest with the human body.

Selira yelled, "Parth, use your dagger. Till then, I will think of something."

"There is no time to think!" I protested taking out my dagger. I kept running forward, looked back and threw the dagger in the Trosun's eye. The aim was perfect. The beast howled with pain and sat on the ground.

I stopped and panted heavily. But in that time, the Minotaur recovered and threw the dagger back at me. It fell some steps in front of me. I took it up and kept it back in my belt.

Just then, Selira shouted, "Parth, bring that monster towards me," she paused and then said to herself, "I have thought of a new move!"

I changed my direction. I took a right turn, then again turned right. This way I took a U-turn. This was just like the game *'Temple Run'*.

Selira was waiting for me on a large branch of a tree with a sword in her hand.

I said while running, "What will you do now?"

"You just keep running. I will try my best!" she said nervously.

When the monster was just three metres away from that tree, Selira jumped on his chest with her sword held tightly in front of her face. She thrust the sword into the beast's chest and landed on the ground.

The Trosun fell with such force, that it shook the whole ground. At first, we thought that he was dead but he got up and went behind Selira. He was roaring so loudly that I thought my eardrums would blast.

Suddenly, I remembered something. The pen which killed that Ligon was in my pocket. I pulled it out and pointed it towards the monster. Nothing happened! Then I understood that the crystal should be pointed towards the monster. I turned the pen and pointed it towards the Trosun with a jerk.

The Ligon was only a small animal but this Minotaur was three times bigger than that. I needed more power to kill him. The pen was giving out rays of blue light. Then, with a blinding flash, there was a blast and the monster went flying towards a big tree. The tree was uprooted and the monster was dead.

The blast was so strong that I was thrown backwards and was unconscious for five minutes. When I woke up, Selira was standing besides that beast. She looked stunned. There was a big hole in the stomach of that beast.

She jumped and said, "We killed a real, big Minotaur!" Then she ran towards me and said, "That pen is *awesome*. We can reach that fortress very easily!"

I got up and said, "Okay, okay! Can you take this pen for some time?" I handed her that pen. I could feel something crawling on my back. I took off my jacket and handed it also to Selira.

Suddenly, something big jumped behind me and before I could look back, it swallowed me. I was in total darkness. It was unbelievable. It looked as if our quest had ended with me in the stomach of a giant monster!

□

13
Diomedes[5]

I was covered in darkness. Even my jacket and pen were not with me. I was about to lose hope when some light came in. I looked up. The light stayed for some time and then vanished. I felt myself covered in some sticky substance.

Then, Selira's voice came through. She was screaming, "Parth... are you alive or this monster has made a soup of you?"

"I am alive!! Please help me!" I yelled.

"But what should I do? This monster is invincible!" she yelled back.

I quickly replied, "Use that pen. It will kill this monster!"

After a few seconds, her voice entered the dark place, "Yes, but if I use that pen, then you will also be blasted off along with this beast."

I said to myself, "Well, yes! I never thought of that!"

---

5. Diomedes: A Greek powerful landlord who lived in a rugged section on the shores of black sea. He murdered the local ruler and stole his lands. He was killed by his own man eater horses when Heracles threw him in front of their trough.

This conversation of ours was going on with me bouncing up and down inside the stomach of that beast. Just then, something pointy pricked my chin. I felt what it was. The pointy thing was the tip of the Madges. I remembered what Mr. Clapperton had told me about it. This thought gave me an idea.

I called out to Selira, "Selira... use that pen now. I will survive!"

• "But what if...whoa... what if you get hurt?"she was probably on a tree as her voice seemed a little higher.

"Just use it!!" I shouted and pulled the Madges of my shirt. After some time, she replied, "Okay, as you wish!!" And a few seconds later, "Here...you...GO!!!"

Just as she finished the last word, the stomach of that creature pierced open. I covered my face with my hand. I felt a lot of pressure on my chest where that Madges was.

Then, everything was silent. After opening my eyes and looking around, I saw that I was lying inside the open stomach of a hellhound as if it was a bed. I quickly got out and Earth felt like a cushion.

Something hot touched my chest. I looked down and removed the Madges in a flash. The chain attached to it was also hot. I threw it on the ground. Its inside was filled with a blue smoke just like the one I had seen in the Uniball. After a few minutes, its upper part melted and only a flat triangle remained. I touched it and surprisingly, it was cool. I wore it back.

Selira started to come towards me but stopped after a few steps. "You look horrible!" she said at last, looking at me from top to bottom.

I was covered in the blood and saliva of that hellhound. "I know! Is there any river nearby?"

"Well, yes! I saw some water when I was on top of that tree," she pointed towards a tall tree on our left. "By the way, how did you survive?"

"This Madges has the ability to protect us from any hard strike but only once. That is how I survived!" I explained.

We walked further on. My blue t-shirt was totally ruined. It was torn from many places and the condition of my jeans was even worse. Its lower side was torn and it was completely wet.

After walking for about five minutes, we found a big pond. I told Selira to wait for me behind a tree and to keep her eyes away from me.

I bathed heartily for thirty minutes. Selira kept asking whether I had bathed completely and my answer was 'no'. It was good that my previous shirt and jeans were dry.

When I had finished, I called out to Selira, "Hey Selira, come on. I am finished."

Selira was cross with me. So she said, "Now, you wait here and I will have a bath!" She handed me the pen, the jacket and my backpack.

I waited for another thirty minutes behind a tree and then we were ready to go. It was three o'clock and the sun was shining strongly.

I said, "Do we have to cross this river?"

"There is no choice. If we want to reach to the fortress, we have to cross it."

"But, isn't it the same river Kandge?"

"No, no, no, it couldn't be! The Kandge cannot find its way so far underground!" she said half-confidently.

"Okay I agree, but there must be some dangers waiting for us in the river," I said.

"We have to take a risk," Selira stared at the cold river for some time. "Come on, let us make a raft. But first let us have some food. I'm very hungry." We had to take food rationally after that lunch as our food supplies were finishing.

So, we made a raft, whole evening and slept at night. A very unusual thing happened at night. I had a dream just like the one which I had before coming to Florencia. This time, Prime Unicorn came in my dream.

I was standing in the Uni-chamber and the box which kept the Uniball was open. The Prime Unicorn was looking at it. Then, he turned towards me and said, "Parth, remember that every person in this world dies some day. No one can become immortal. In your mythologies also, Lord Vishnu took the avatar of 'Narsimha' to kill the demon named 'Hiranyakashyap'. Who knows that God has chosen you for this task? You may also be an avatar for us. Realise your powers!!

"You can kill your enemy and by doing so, your name will be written in golden letters in the history of Florencia. We all depend on you. Believe in yourself!"

Just as he completed, I woke up.

I remembered all that he had said. My attention continuously went to the words 'Narsimha'. I remembered that story. "Wow! I can defeat the enemy about whom Prime Unicorn was talking," I said to myself. Then after a few minutes, my eyes closed and I again went into a dreamless sleep.

We set sail in the day. The river was calm at first but as we reached to its centre, big waves started forming. Then, two big large sharks came from nowhere and ate a big part of the raft.

"What should we do now?" I asked Selira.

She thought for some time and then said, "Parth, I have a plan. Do not use your pen. We will ride them!"

I was flabbergasted. "Are you crazy? They will ride *us* if I avoid the use of this pen!"

"Look, the raft is broken and it will sink soon. Everybody has to die, so why not die with style? And if the luck is good, then we'll survive," Selira said, looking at me in the eyes. I trusted her.

She cut her rope in two parts and tied the head of each rope in a circular shape just as cowboys do. Then, she threw the ropes in the mouth of the sharks. The ropes got stuck in between the nose and mouth of the shark. The sharks tried to get away but Selira held on tightly.

She gave one end of the rope to me and said, "Hold this rope tightly and jump on that shark."

I jumped on the shark uncertainly. Selira was already on her shark.

"Okay, off we go!" she shouted and we surfed towards the other shore.

The small journey was exciting, scary and cool! There was a danger of falling in the water and the shark eating me, but the way water and cold air touched my face, it was superb!

We reached to the shore very quickly. Selira said, "Parth, get ready to jump on the shore."

"What...?" I was not sure about this also.

We jumped on the land. The pain of my ankle returned. The sharks growled and went back.

Selira said, "That was fun!"

"Yeah, it was too much fun!" I said sarcastically. "My ankle is burning with pain. I had removed those leaves which Selira had put on the wound.

"Oh, I'm sorry!" she stopped and then laughed.

After laughing for some time, she said, "The fortress must be somewhere near."

"Shhh...I can hear something!" I whispered.

There was heavy breathing and thudding walks. We hid behind a big bush and saw a beast guarding a door attached to an iron wall.

It was a giant monster with a large club in his hand. Then, I recognised the monster. It was the ferocious, the powerful, the blood-thirsty – Diomedes.

No! *The* Diomedes! It was a Greek monster.

Behind me, Selira gasped. We went back. I said, "Hey, wasn't he killed by his own horses because of Heracles?"

"Yes, but reincarnation is a real thing! The monster reincarnated!"

"He reincarnated?" It was unbelievable. "In India also, the concept of reincarnation is used."

"Every monster does!" she said. "But how is it used in your country?"

"In our epic novel 'Mahabharata', when the hero Parth, as my name is, was not able to fight his own family,"

Selira interrupted, "So are you that Parth?"

"God knows, maybe I am!" I smiled and continued, "Then lord Krishna told him that our body may die, but our *aatma*, or our soul, is immortal. It just changes the body as we change clothes. Our holy script 'Bhagvad Geeta' tells us all this."

"So have you read it?"

"Yes, my grandma told me all this!" I finished and asked again, "You mean that Ligon, Trosun and that hellhound we killed are back?"

"Not so early, but yes, they will be back."

"Oh, great, but let's not waste time and kill that Diomedes," I took out my pen.

"No, we just need to make him unconscious so that the other guards do not get alerted. You go and divert him and I will make him unconscious!" She took out her sword and I kept my pen back into the pocket.

I nodded but it was a very difficult task. With determination, I went in front of him and yelled, "Hey Dio, you ugly rotten brat!"

He looked at me and roared.

I shouted, "There was no need of Heracles. Your horses were enough to kill you! You are a dumb, lazy donkey."

That was enough to make him red with anger. He ran towards me and raised his club. Just then, Selira's sword rested just inches away from him. He looked back at Selira and ran towards her.

I took advantage of this. I picked up the sword and ran towards the beast. Then I forgot everything and slammed the hilt of my sword into the place between the throat and the shoulder of Diomedes.

The beast fell down and unconsciousness surrounded him. Selira was shocked.

Then, she said, "Hey, I wanted to say, the things which you said to this Diomedes were both horrible and fantastic."

I winked at Selira!

□

14
The Centaurs' Fortress

We made the unconscious Diomedes stand by the support of a strong tree and crossed his hands so that nobody would be suspicious. Then, I thought of a pair of sunglasses and they appeared in my pocket. I placed them on Diomedes' closed eyes to cover them. I tried to make him smile but I myself was scared by his ferocious grin.

I asked Selira, "Hey, but Diomedes was such a horrible monster. So, how were the centaurs able to control him?"

"They could've done it probably by a computer chip?" she answered in a questioning way, pointing towards the back of Diomedes' neck.

There was a small black chip stuck behind him.

"The centaurs are very, very intelligent creatures. When they were our friends, they introduced many new inventions and technologies," Selira continued.

I went near the metal door. It was locked and needed a fingerprint scanner.

I said, "It needs a fingerprint scanner. What should we do now?"

"Should we carry that Diomedes to this place? He must be the password!" she said looking towards the leaning Diomedes.

"No, no. It would be very hard to carry him here and it would waste a lot of time," I stopped her.

"Then, I have a plan!" She took out a small mirror from her pocket and took it to Diomedes. She pressed Diomedes' finger on the mirror and came back.

"Here is the password. Take it and press it against that scanner." I took the mirror and pressed it on the scanner. The next moment some words were flashing above us – Welcome to Centauria.

I said, "Well, you're brilliant! I was thinking of cutting his thumb."

Selira smiled and said, "Yes, that is a good idea, but it is a bit... bloody!! Now, you should keep your backpack on a branch of that tree," she pointed towards a small tree. "It is wet and will not be of much use now!"

I agreed and hung the bag on that branch. While Selira fastened her shoelace, I took my smartphone out of my jacket to check if it was damaged or not but it worked perfectly. Then, I kept it back in. We pressed the button from which the door opened. In front of us, there was huge mirror in which we could see ourselves clearly.

Selira removed a twig from her hairs and said, "What should we do now? This door is nothing?"

"There's got to be a way!" I kept my hand on the mirror and my hand went towards the other side. I looked at Selira and raised my eyebrows.

"Yes, there is a way!" she said and we entered into the fortress.

This place was nothing like Florencia. It was a small town. It was surrounded by tall metal walls and there were only centaurs. No unicorns, no humans! Everyone was in the outfit of a warrior. It looked as if they were preparing for a war, probably against Florencia.

Selira whispered into my ear, "We need to hide somewhere! They haven't yet noticed us. Quick!"

We stayed behind carts, vehicles and statues. Then, we entered into a small house. Its residents were not there but the door was open. So, we went inside the house. In one room of that house, there was a centaur boy. He was about to scream, but Selira covered his mouth with her hand.

She said, "Don't scream. Calm down! We are your friends. Tell me what your name is?"

The boy looked at us for a minute and then stammered slowly, "My n...name is Tromes."

"Okay, Tromes! Can you help us?" Selira asked hopefully.

"What help do you want from me?" The boy was less scared now.

"I want to know the place where your commander lives!"

I was standing beside a door all this time, just listening to their conversation.

Tromes said, "I can teleport you there! He lives in a fort which is underground."

"Really, But how?"

"I have a machine which can teleport you there! Actually, our commander is a very mysterious person. Come on now, follow me!"

He took us to the basement of the house. There was a machine with a lot of buttons and two elevators.

Selira came towards me, "Parth, this was so easy! We will reach there without any problem. Come on!"

I spoke for the first time, "Selira, I don't think something is right here!" I raised my voice, "Hey Tromes, I've read that you need to fill in the name of the place where you want to go in a teleporting machine. But you have not filled any name!"

"Oh, y...yes, I f...forgot." He typed in the name – CENT-FORT."Now, both of you get in those lifts!"

Selira stepped into the elevator. I got into another one. Tromes pressed a button and the doors of the machine closed. They were made of hard glass.

"This blue button teleports you..." His face broke into a wicked smile. "...But this red button traps you!"

We realised that he had lied! He turned out to be a fraud.

Selira was very angry. "You, betrayer, liar, you cheated us!"

"I never lied! We are faithful to our commander. We can give our life, but never betray the commander!" He pressed the red button and a coating of iron was spread onto that glass. There were slits through which we could see. Tromes ran out to call other centaurs.

"Parth, use your pen! Get us out of here!" Selira said.

I took out the pen from my pocket and blasted the iron. Then, I opened Selira's lift and she got out. I said, "Look, this teleporter is the only way through which we can go to that underground fort."

"But we don't know how to operate it!"

I thought for some time and said, "Hey, that boy said that this blue button teleports us. Come on!"

"But what if the boy had lied?"

"I don't know. We have to take the chances! If those centaurs find us, they will probably throw us in front of some beast."

"Yes, that is right!"

"You go and stand in that lift and I'll press this button!" I said.

"And when will you come?" she looked at me.

"I'll come after you!" I pushed the button and waited for some time. Nothing happened.

"He lied to us!" Selira clenched her teeth.

"No, the machine is saying that an error has occurred! I think it needs a key." There was a slit in the button also! I looked around.

"He must've taken the key with him!" I said.

"I have another plan!" She took out a hairpin from her pocket and inserted it in the button. She had never used that hairpin before! We could hear the hoof steps of the centaurs!

She turned the pin and a message flashed on the screen – Teleporter Unlocked. It was just like I had seen in detective movies.

Selira said, "Come inside this lift and I will press this button!"

She pressed the blue button and we ran inside the lift. We squeezed and went down just as the other centaurs entered into the room.

In five seconds, we were in front of a large and dark fort. Our final adventure had begun!

□

15
The Enemy

We entered into the fort. There were many passageways. The entire place was lit by torches burning on every corner. The centaur boy Tromes had lied that the fort was underground. Actually, only the entrance of that fort was underground. The rest of it was going upwards towards the sky.

When we reached near the gate of the fort, a mechanical voice said – 'Please enter the password'.

I said to Selira, "What should we do now? Why everything needs a password?"

"Look what is written there. I think it's a kind of riddle which gives the password!" She pointed to the top of that door.

There were two lines written on it –

A centaur combines with a unicorn;
Florencia, from thread to thread, will be torn.

"Not a very sensible riddle!" Selira said.

So, we needed to solve this riddle! There was a screen near the gate. It said that we had three chances to type the correct option.

Selira said, "I will fill in the name. It says that a centaur mixes with a unicorn! So, the password must be – "

She typed in – "Centorn". The screen flashed – WRONG. She typed again. This time she typed a new name – "Tauruni". It was also wrong!

Then, I realised the password. Selira was going to type again but I stopped her and wrote – "Unitaur". That was the correct password as the screen flashed – CORRECT, WELCOME.

The gate opened slowly. Selira was looking at me with wide eyes. She asked, "Did you know the password?"

"No, I saw your last name, Tauruni, and just exchanged the words!"

"But why did you change it?"

"Because unicorns are the more powerful creatures than centaurs and the centaurs are more proud, so they will always keep their name first in this riddle!" I said.

"You're an intelligent boy!" she said.

My cheeks were becoming red, so I said, "Okay, come on! We have to finish our mission!" We went in and the door closed behind us.

We were standing before a very big castle. There were hundreds of cannons on its topmost floor. How will the centaurs use these cannons when half of the fort is underground? – I thought.

Selira took my hand and shoved me behind a statue of a centaur. I asked, "What happened?"

"Shhh, someone is coming!" she whispered.

There were three centaurs coming towards the gate. They just talked and went out. We entered into the castle. There were swords, spears, bows, arrows, shields. They were preparing for a very deadly battle.

We came over a fork. There were four passageways in all directions. Suddenly, four centaurs came from all the four passageways and put their swords on our throat.

Selira was ready to fight but I whispered to her, "We need to see their commander! This is the only way and we don't know this castle also. So, don't attack them!"

"You made a mistake by coming here. Our commander will have you and your foolish friend executed!" One of the centaurs said.

Selira let out an angry grunt. We turned left and walked straight. There was a big lift and we went even deeper in the ground. I guessed that there was some kind of practising arena there as noises of metal clanking against metal and battle noises were coming from that place.

When we entered into the arena, I understood what Unitaur stood for. It was the name of their commander! He was half unicorn and half centaur.

The lower part of his body (the horse's part) was white just like a unicorn. From top, he had the body of a human and he had a unicorn's horn on his head. He had long black hairs and a muscular body. He was fighting with the robot of a centaur.

The four centaurs, who brought us here, said, "Sir, here are the children!"

He kept fighting for some time and suddenly inserted his horn in the chest of that robot. Then, he slashed the robot's head with the sword which he was holding. The robot fell down. He turned back. I saw his face and was stunned. He was Sam! His face was of Sam's! Those green eyes and long nose, everything was same! The only difference was that he appeared to be the older version of Sam.

When he saw me, he said, "Oh, my best friend, Parth! Isn't it a long time since we've met? How are you? Why didn't you tell me about your new friend?" He looked at Selira who was standing behind me.

His voice was as if two voices were speaking at the same time. He smiled wickedly and said, "Are you stunned to see me in this body? I was also stunned when I saw myself!"

He waved his hand and the centaurs left the room. I was shocked till now. Selira asked, "Do you know him?"

I nodded. "Can you tell me how?" She asked again.

I shook my head. "Why?" She made an angry sound.

"I will tell you why I am here!" The Unitaur started, "That Prime Unicorn and I, we started together. We both were very good friends. We were equal, but… now look where am I and where is he!"

Behind me, Selira joked, "Yes, you are very low and he is very high!" She giggled on her pun but I was still shocked.

He looked at Selira with a cold stare. Selira stopped giggling. "You and your friend are nothing before me! You both are going to die!"

I pleaded, "Sam, please! Revenge is not the solution to all the problems. We will help you. Tell us your problem and…."

He yelled, "Do *not* call me Sam! There *was* no Sam, there is only Unitaur!"

"B…but you were my friend!" I was shocked. How can he trick me? – I thought.

"You've still not understood?" He started laughing. "I've tricked you, you foolish boy! I learned that a boy was coming to that town. So, I tried to be your friend. When you first asked me about that white light, I knew that you were the chosen one as that idiot Stan was watching you."

"Even that Prime Unicorn didn't know that I was with you! You kept telling me all those incidents and dreams! I was the one who sent you into that forest! When you came back, I knew that you had met with the unicorns!" He laughed again.

"Was your mother also a lie?" I asked.

"Yes, she was one of the centaur ladies! But now, the time has come to conquer Florencia!"

"But how will you do it? Half of your fort is underground!" Selira said.

"You brainless girl, I will take this whole fort to the battle-ground! I will instruct my people to move out of the city and then my fort will come out. I've waited for ten years! I will not stop now!" He roared.

"But how did you steal the power of Uniball?" I tried to get as much information out of him as I could.

"I just took five powerful unicorns, cut their horns and used them to steal it!" He smiled wickedly.

He was so cruel, cunning and insane! I asked him, "And were all those traps and monsters yours?"

"Yes I needed them to bring people to me! I have all the people with me!"

This meant that Selira's parents were still alive. I asked angrily, "What did you do to them?"

"Oh, I just destroyed their brains and fitted an artificial brain in their heads!" He answered with an evil smile.

After hearing this, Selira sat on the ground, tears coming down her cheeks. Unitaur called the four centaurs, "Ledge, Cander, Bandera, Procter! Take these children to prison. They will see the end of Florencia!"

The four centaurs carried us and threw us into the prison. I looked at Selira and tried to comfort her.

She wiped her tears and said in a determined voice, "I will save my parents at every cost, no matter I live or die!"

□

16
The Unitaur's Secret

We were sitting on a bench in that Unitaur's prison. I had told her everything about Sam. I was still not able to believe that Sam was my enemy. Selira was silent. I said, "We will find your parents soon."

"But for that, we need to get out of this prison. Take out your pen. I want to find my parents faster than ever," she said with a hint of anger.

I said, "No, if we break out of here, the centaurs will get alert and will try to find us. We need something to cut these bars," I pointed to the door of the prison. "And then after we get out, we'll put those bars back!"

"Yeah, as if nothing had happened. But we don't have any sharp thing. All my weapons are taken by them and your pen only blasts or kills!" She said.

"Only if I can control its power, I will be able to turn it into a sword!"

"But that is impossible. You've seen its power. We had *killed* the Trosun with it! If you will try to do it, you yourself can get blown to pieces!"

"Everything is possible if we have the will to attain it," I got up from the bench.

I concentrated on the pen, its power! I stopped blinking and held the pen more tightly. I had to block all my thoughts. Suddenly, a surge of warm power went from my hand to my heart. My eyes got closed. At first, I felt as if I was going to blast off. The power was so strong that my legs left the ground and when I opened my eyes, I was standing in mid-air!

Selira's eyes widened. She stammered, "P…Parth, y…you are fl…flying!"

In an instant, I fell back on the ground. A centaur guard came running towards our cell, "What happened? Why is that boy lying on the ground?"

Selira said quickly, "He is having pain in his leg!"

The guard glared at me angrily and went back. I looked up at Selira and said, "I am connected! I can control its power now!"

She said with a smile, "Show me a proof!"

I held the pen in front of me and concentrated on its crystal. In the beginning, some sparks were produced and then a ray of blue light came out. The pen looked like a sword now!

Selira exclaimed, "Cool! You're truly special!"

I smiled and carefully made a circle in those bars. We took out the bars and came out after replacing them back. Selira's weapons were kept just outside the cell. So, she took them. We made the guard unconscious and locked him in a cell.

We came out and looked at the corridors. They were loaded with guards. I had an idea.

I took out the compass and told Selira, "You take this compass and rescue your parents. I will go on my own." I pointed to the button on the bottom of that compass, "Just press this button and you'll get invisible."

She tried to protest but afterwards understood. She hugged me and pressed the button. We both got invisible but she was still visible to me. I was very surprised when she hugged me.

Then I gave her those marbles which could blast off and we got separated. I crossed all the corridors as I remembered the way through which we had arrived at those prisons. I took the lift and went down to the practising arena. I wanted to know why Sam betrayed all of us.

I reached there and hid behind the door. Though I was invisible but still that Unitaur was very cunning and I didn't know his powers. He was angry with someone and was screaming at him.

He yelled, "How could you lose it? I should not have given this work to you!"

The centaur said, "I…It suddenly started changing its form and fell into the river Kandge. We…we were afraid to go there as it was dawn!"

"And you are telling me this now, when I am only an inch close to my victory! I don't need any coward in my army!" He took out a golden rod from behind him, which I had not seen before, and pointed it towards the centaur. A dark blue light was produced and the centaur vaporised.

Suddenly he looked towards me and the door got closed. I became visible. I was stunned but quickly recollected. I took out my dagger and threw it at him. It was going straight to his chest but suddenly it stopped and fell on the ground.

His rod was glowing and somehow I got stuck on the wall behind me.

He said, "Oh, we meet again! I know you want to know why I want to conquer Florencia! I will tell you myself as your death is very near."

"I and that Prime Unicorn grew as very best friends We both had equal powers but I had one quality. I was braver than him. I had saved him many times from different monsters. Even when elections for the Prime Unicorn were held, we both were chosen." For the first time, Sam's voice became single.

Then, as fast as the change had come, it went away. "But, when Uniball chose Warner, I was broken. At every turn of life, we were equal. Then why was he considered superior than me?" The Unitaur was becoming angry.

"I decided to steal Uniball. When I went into that Uni-chamber, the Uniball made me like this! A complete freak! I understood that the Uniball cannot be uprooted from its chamber. I took the help of those five unicorns and stole a part of the power of the Uniball."

He held out that rod for me to see it. On top of that rod was a hollow, transparent sphere. Inside it, there was a small, blue cubicle. It was connected to that sphere with hundreds of current like rays. It appeared to be a larger version of an atom.

Unitaur said, "Do you want to see its power?"

He pointed it towards a bronze statue. The statue melted. He once again pointed the rod towards the melted bronze. The bronze became gold and a statue of the Unitaur was formed.

He laughed wickedly, "Now, my friend Parth! You know everything except my secret!"

"And what is that?" I hoped that I sounded brave. My hands were aching horribly.

He smiled, "A secret should not be told, you dumb boy! And...I don't want anybody to know my secrets. So, you must die!" He pointed that rod towards me but stopped.

"I forgot to tell you the name of my weapon. It is called the Unirod! When I take Uniball, its centre of power will be stored in this! I will have the world's deadliest and most powerful weapon!" he laughed again.

Then, he pointed the rod towards me again, this time without stopping. I closed my eyes but felt nothing. Was death like this?

I slowly opened my eyes and saw that the whole power was coming towards me, but was absorbed by an invisible shield. Only the outline of the shield could be seen.

Unitaur stopped. He looked at me, then at his Unirod. The shield had vanished. Then, with a flash of realisation, he said, "No, no, it couldn't be!"

□

17

The Secret of the Pen

The Unitaur ran towards me. "Tell me! Do you have any power of the Uniball? Tell me!" He said and searched my pockets frantically. I could feel the pen in my inner pocket but when the Unitaur reached near it, it vanished and reappeared in my outer pocket.

He again searched my all the pockets and probably he felt the pen as he said, "You can't play with me!"

He took a step back and held his Unirod in front of him. Suddenly, my whole jacket started burning and I was damned. I was burning but still was not burning. I managed to speak between flames, "Gi... give it... it to hi...him, Pl...please." Just as I finished, the pen dropped down from the jacket.

The Unitaur stopped and smiled cunningly. He picked up the pen. My jacket had protected me from the fire and again was in its old form.

"Now you have no powers left!!" He clenched his teeth. First he studied the pen for one minute and then held it near to his Unirod. There were some sparks produced and then very faint bonds could be seen.

"Yes, yes, I got it! Now, even the strongest force in the universe cannot defeat me!" he said. "I wonder why it took this form!"

"Give it back, its mine! It does not contain any power of Uniball." I was not sure of this.

He said, "You silly boy, you yourself are not sure about this!" He laughed for some time and then called a centaur, "Procter! Take this brat to our most advanced cell and also catch that friend of his! I'm going to my laboratory, so don't disturb me!" And he went away.

The centaur which had brought me and Selira here was Procter. He grabbed my elbow and started to take me to their 'most advanced cell'.

I tried to make him talk. I asked, "Are you one of those centaurs which brought us here?"

He nodded.

I continued, "Do you know we faced how many monsters before coming here? We should get something more than this!"

"What more do you want?" he scowled.

"Maybe you can tell me where that laboratory of your commander is?" I asked. I hoped that he would not guess my trick.

"No! Even if I tell you that it is on the topmost floor, what will you do?" That centaur was so foolish! And Prime Unicorn had told me that centaurs were very intelligent!

"I can make you unconscious and run to that laboratory!" I said.

"How will you make me unconscious?" He seemed confused.

In that time, I took out two marbles from my pocket and threw them in his face. "This is how I made you unconscious!" I said and he fell on the ground.

I took his hand and dragged him back to the lift. That Procter was so heavy! We got out of that lift and I strapped him to a pillar which was in the darkest corner of the arena. I took his sword and went upwards through the lift. The topmost floor was the eighth floor.

When I reached to the terrace (the floor was actually the terrace!), a centaur was coming towards me. The good thing was that he had not seen me. The bad thing was that if he saw me, I would be completely trapped and he was coming towards the lift! I needed to do something fast. Then an idea occurred to me!

I hid behind the lift door. When the centaur came in, I slammed the hilt of my sword in his head. He also was unconscious. How many times do I have to do this? – I thought.

It was night time. We had spent a day in this city!

I dragged the centaur to a corner and went into the lab. I didn't see anyone. There was no one there. The whole terrace was empty! Then I spotted it. A door was just opposite to the door from which I had entered. It was hidden by many shelves of chemicals and other things.

I went there. Some voices were coming from behind that door. First voice was of the Unitaur. "I want it fast doctor!"

A second voice came, "I am doing it fast! You don't want any mistake, do you?"

I pushed the gate one or two centimetres ahead. I now saw what was happening. There were two people there. They had removed the crystal of my pen and were draining out the energy from it.

The energy was kept in another container. The Unitaur was taking out power from that container into his Unirod. The other person whom Sam had called the doctor was taking out energy from my pen. He was not a centaur. I was not able to see his face.

I opened the gate some more and saw the doctor. He was a human with white hairs. His face looked familiar. Then I remembered him. He was the same shopkeeper from whom I had bought that smart phone.

I realised that he had tricked me. While selling that phone, he had fitted a transmitter on me. That was why the Unitaur always knew where I was even when I was invisible.

Can I trust anyone here except Selira? – I wondered. I searched my entire body but wasn't able to find that tracer. Then a thought struck me. I took out that smartphone and tried to switch it off. A message flashed – Cannot switch off the phone. The transmitter is on. I went out and threw the phone from the railing. The phone went down with lot of speed and when it touched the ground, nothing was left of it!

I went back to the lab. The doctor was saying something but I only heard a part of it, "...Power will be yours, master!"

Suddenly, there was a loud beep somewhere and the Unitaur said, "What happened? Is your tracer alright?"

"No, it's destroyed and he is somewhere near!"

"What, this means that he again escaped. I'll have to do something about that brat," the Unitaur said.

I knew that they were talking about me! I stepped back. The man opened the door very fast and I fell on the floor. He smiled at me with evil expressions.

"Oh, It feels good to see you again, Parth! How are you?" he said.

"You are a trickster! I thought you were trying to help but..." There was no need to say anything further. I was feeling very bad.

"I don't want any obstacle in my path. Kill that boy, doctor! He has been irritating me since the moment he came here." He started to carry on with his work of inserting my pen's power in his Unirod.

The man took a metal rod which was kept on a table and was about to hit me on the head, but I quickly took out a hand full of marbles from my jacket and threw them on his chest.

The doctor fell back. I got up and slammed the hilt of my sword in his chest. He was already weakened from the last attack and this one made him lose his senses.

I ran towards the Unitaur. I said, "Give me my pen back!" That was a foolish thing to say!

"Yeah, as if you'd say and I'll do it! This pen was more powerful than my weapon but now their power is equal. Soon, my Unirod will have more power," he said. "My Unirod was incomplete without this power. I was searching for this power and now I have got it. I am completed now!!"

I stopped. "But whose power is in that pen?" I was totally confused and angry.

He looked astonished, "You've still not understood? And here I thought how you killed all those monsters which I sent!"

"Tell me whose power is in that pen?" I knew the answer but it seemed better to hear it from his mouth.

He stopped his work and kept a hand on his Unirod. Then, he pointed the hand towards me and I was thrown out of that room. He had applied a lot of power but I had ducked and had my head banged against a metallic table. The table fell over me. The Unitaur came out of that lab and ensured that I was unconscious.

He said, "Yes, now this problem is also finished. No one can stop me now." He started going but stopped and, with a despicable stare and a wicked smile, said, "It has the stolen power of...Uniball!" Then he went back into his lab and everything went black.

□

18

The Rescuer Selira

At that time, Selira came to the terrace. She looked happy but when she saw me, she again wore that worried expression. She ran towards me and shook me very dangerously. I opened my eyes. She asked, "What happened? And why were you lying down?"

"He attacked me and I was almost dead, but... somehow I survived. I think even god is with me. You tell me, did you rescue all the people?"

Selira quickly told me how she saved the other people:

"After separating, I went to the other prisons. As I was invisible, I went there without any hiding. There were three prisons. In the first two, there were lots of people but in the third one, there was only one person and that too was a centaur.

I first went to the door and made the two guards unconscious. Then I pressed the button of that compass and became visible. I went to the prisons and dropped one each marble on their locks.

My parents were not in those people who were free. The centaur didn't come out from the third cell. I went in there.

I asked, "Sir, all the other people are outside, so why are you still inside?"

"Because being in this prison is my destiny and I don't want my soldiers to see me like this again," he answered. He looked as if he was about to cry.

I questioned, "If they are your soldiers, then... who are you sir?"

"I was the true ruler of Centauria, but that Unitaur made my soldiers rebel against me. I would never start a war with Florencia but he is evil!"

I was shocked to see him in this state. I said to him, "Sir, we can help you. We are here to defeat that Unitaur."

"It is impossible unless you have the power of Uniball itself!" He turned back towards the wall.

I decided to forget everything and come straight to the point. "Can you tell me where are those people whose minds he had destroyed?"

"He has not destroyed the minds of any people. He has fitted a controlling chip in their brains. They are now his slaves and if you want to rescue them, you need to shut off their chips."

I was relieved to hear this.

The king continued, "They are in a big hall where they are making weapons for the Unitaur. The hall is on the fourth floor at the end of the corridor."

A tear dropped down from my eye but I quickly wiped it and asked, "How do you know all this?"

"I broke out from the prison but was caught!" he answered.

"Is there a way or a vehicle through which I can send them to a safer place?" I asked hopefully.

"Yes, there is a plane hidden inside this fort. I made it myself."

"But what if the Unitaur has discovered it?"

"No, it is hidden in a secret place. No one can find it except me!"

"Great!! But sir, we need you to guide us. Please, can you help us?" I asked.

He said, "Yes, but I cannot fight that Unitaur." Now, he came out of the prison.

"You don't need to fight with him. I want you to guide these people." I pointed to the other people who were listening to our conversation. "I want you to take them to that plane. I will reach there soon with the other people!"

"Yes, I will take these people there. You should rescue them and shut off their chips. I wish you best of luck!"

I started to go but he took my hand and gave me a piece of paper. "This will help you. Now you should go!"

I smiled at him and went to the fourth floor. In the way, I saw those four centaurs that brought us here, quickly became invisible and just went by them. The hall was at the end of the corridor.

When I entered into the hall, my eyes widened. There were hundreds of people in that hall and everybody was striking a hammer on a piece of metal to form a sword. The noise was ear-piercing.

I looked around and spotted them. My mother and father were sitting together. I ran near them. I wished that they could see me but I was invisible. I tried very hard not to cry but my eyes were not in my control.

I wanted to hug them but this mission was more important.

I saw a controlling centre behind a wall of glass. I went there and saw a door at the corner. I entered into it. There was one guard at the door and two were watching the working people through the glass.

There was also a control panel behind them attached to the wall. One centaur was on the control panel. So, totally there were four centaurs. I needed to do everything silently.

The centaur on the control panel was playing some game. So, I decided to make him unconscious first. I went near him and slammed the handle of my sword on his shoulder. He made a low grunt, "Unh!!!" It was barely audible.

The other centaur asked, "What happened, Laurie? Have you lost the game again?"

I made a hum and made his face look into the other direction. It was good that he was standing by the support of the wall. So, when he went limp, I had to do no hard work.

Then, I went outside the gate and made a noise. When the guard came out, I made him unconscious too. I went in and made one of the centaurs lose his senses.

The other one looked scared. He was about to press the alarm button but I went near him and striked him onto the head.

I became visible again and went to the control panel. It was super-confusing. There were so many buttons. I looked onto every button but wasn't able to find any shut down button.

Then, I spotted it. A very small button located on a corner of the control panel. I pressed it and suddenly the noise of the hammer stopped. I looked towards the people. Everybody was getting up from their places and was watching their surroundings.

My parents were together and were confused. I went out of that controlling centre and told all those people, "Everybody listen to me, you were trapped here. Now we need to get out. You all touch me and I will make everyone invisible. We will go away from here."

Probably my mom and dad had not seen me. We all became invisible. I had not asked the king that where was that plane. Then, I remembered that piece of paper which the king had given me.

I took it out and opened it. There was written – The plane is behind the practising arena on the underground floor. Pull the hand of the statue and you will find the way.

I lead all the people to the practising arena and saw a statue of a centaur. I pulled its hand and instantly the wall besides it shifted and a way became visible. There was an extra large plane.

I made everyone visible and said, "Sir, please transport all of them to Florencia safely."

"Yes and I will also tell the Prime Unicorn about that Unitaur attacking them!"

"Thanks!" I said and then I found you here. Selira finished the story.

□

19
The Final Battle

I said, "You did a great job, but I have a very big problem. The Unitaur is stealing my pen's power."

"And why is he stealing that?" I told her the full story of what happened with me.

"The pen contains the power of the Uniball." I informed her.

"This means that we came all the way here, facing monsters just to know that we had the power with us!" Selira said.

"Yes, but now, we can't just sit here and do nothing. We need to fight him," I said.

"We'll do it!" We quietly sneaked into that lab and Selira took out her sword and threw it at that ball. The throw was accurate and the ball blew up. The power went back into my pen. Its crystal again got attached to it.

The Unitaur was surprised to see me. He looked up and said angrily, "You are still alive? I'll kill you now!" He glared at Selira and said, "You two rats are going to fight me?" He started laughing.

He pointed his Unirod angrily towards Selira. A ray of light flashed and Selira was thrown into the wall which was behind us. She fell down and was unconscious.

I was very angry. Then, I remembered my dream with prime unicorn and was filled with a new determination. I said, "We just came here even when we had the power of the Uniball. Now we will not die here, I will fight!"

I ran towards him and jumped on the table, then on his chest with full force. The Unitaur went back a few steps. I landed on the floor, took my pen and ran towards Selira. She was still unconscious.

Suddenly the Unitaur yelled, "Nothing will come between me and my revenge!"

He pointed his Unirod towards me and gave it a strong jerk. A very big ray of light came towards me. I ducked just when the ray passed over me. The energy fell on the door and the wall behind us. I looked back. A very big crack was forming in that wall. I looked upwards and the roof stumbled and fell on us.

I pointed my pen upwards and instantly a shield was formed, stopping the stones from falling on me. I looked towards Selira. The stones were falling on her also.

I thought nothing and pointed the pen towards Selira. She was saved. My hand was held as a shield above me and I waited for the stones to fall. But, for some reason, the stones were also not falling on me. I looked upwards and saw that my hand was acting as a big shield. This was incredible!

The Unitaur was also confused. I threw all the stones on that Unitaur. He held his Unirod in front of him and, suddenly, every stone froze, and then became sand.

While he was doing all this, I ran towards Selira. She had gained consciousness. I said, "Selira, come on! We need to run!"

We came out on the terrace. The Unitaur was behind us. He said, "Don't think that I only have this much power. Here is my little secret!"

Suddenly he spread his *wings*!

"He has wings?!!" Selira said.

How many surprises will we be getting? – I thought.

The Unitaur flew up high in the air. His wings were large and white. That was why they mixed in his skin. I gave Selira those marbles and said, "When that Unitaur comes near us, throw these marbles on his wings. He will not be able to fly!"

"Yeah, this is a good plan!" She showed me thumbs up sign and got ready to blast the Unitaur's wings.

The Unitaur came towards me but stopped and said, "Do you want to know why I am like this? The Uniball made me a combination of a centaur, a unicorn, a human and a griffin! I was very upset at first but soon learned that this was not a curse, it was a boon, it was my power. Now you know too much so you must die!" He threw all the energy of the Unirod at me.

I held my pen in front of me and the shield was formed again which covered me from every side. Somehow, my whole body felt like full of energy, which was fighting the Unitaur. I was feeling involved in this battle. The energy of the Unirod was not able to touch me, but its flow was so strong that I fell on the floor. After some time, the floor gave way and I fell even more down.

I tried to remember how many floors this fort had. It had eight floors with the one underground. The

Unitaur stopped only when I had broken all the eight of them and had made a big hole in that practising arena. My back was burning with pain and my pen fell from my hand. It was good that I had that shield on, or else my backbone would have been smashed by now.

I got up very painfully. The Unitaur came in front of me in a second. I looked up and saw Selira hidden behind a pile of stones on the ground floor.

I signaled her by my eyes. Suddenly the Unitaur leaped towards me with his wings wide open. Here was Selira's chance. I stepped back and fell in the hole which I had created.

Selira took this moment and threw all the marbles on his wings. Her aim was perfect. The marbles blasted off his wings with hundreds of large feathers falling on the ground. The Unitaur howled with pain and fell on the ground with his Unirod.

I got up holding my back. The Unitaur's eyes were closed as if he was unconscious. I said to Selira, "Hey, I think that this Unitaur is unconscious. You should come here!"

Selira said, "Yeah, we won so easily!" She went back towards the elevator.

I looked down on the Unitaur. His eyes opened in a flash and he said, "Not so fast!" He pointed the Unirod towards me.

I stepped back, stumbled because of a stone and fell again. The ray of light shot upwards and the roof stumbled. I quickly crawled towards the door after grabbing my pen.

All the stones fell on that Unitaur. Now only his human part was visible. I looked at him.

"Please help me!" His voice became single and his face was of that innocent Sam. I had to save him. My pen fell from my hand as I ran back to get him out.

Suddenly, his face distorted and he again became that evil Unitaur. He tightly grabbed my hand and directed his Unirod towards me. I picked up a stone with my free hand and threw it on his face. He fell back and the remaining stones on the ceiling fell on him. Selira came from behind me. She had my backpack which I had left outside. A centaur and Stan were with her. I guessed that this centaur was the centaur king. I was happy that Stan was here. After all, he was the first unicorn whom I had met.

"Hey Parth, how are you?" he said.

We started to go. I started towards the door. The stones behind me shifted a little. I looked back. Nothing happened. I moved towards the door.

Suddenly, the Unitaur emerged from beneath the stones. The stones flew everywhere. He again had his wings and looked as strong as he was in the beginning. We all were shocked to see him. He jumped on me and tried to strangle me. I don't know why but I grabbed his horn and applied my full strength. It suddenly broke off. The Unitaur roared with pain and released me. I stabbed the horn in his chest, then again took it out and stabbed him. After doing so for three-four times, I remembered that he was Sam – my friend. I stopped and took a step back. Sam fell on the floor and continuously howled with pain.

Selira said, "Parth, kill him, quickly! Use your pen."

"He is not completely dead. Only you can kill him." Stan said from behind me. "He'll reincarnate. Before that, destroy him and release him from this pain."

"No, I cannot do this, he is my friend!" I said.

"No Parth, there was no Sam. He tricked you. All our efforts will be in vain. Do it, Parth do it!" Selira encouraged me.

I picked up the pen and pointed it down on the Unitaur. He burned and burned and burned. A different, warm light was produced and the whole arena was filled with that pen's light. This was the end of him.

Behind me, The Centaur king said, "It is written in bible that God said, 'Let there be light,' and there was light. God saw that the light was good, and He separated the light from the darkness. God called the light "day", and the darkness he called "night." And there was evening, and there was morning—the first day."

"Yes, and this is the first day after the destruction of evil. A new light will shine and every person will be purified by this light!" Stan added as if in a trance.

The Unitaur's body became a centaur, then a unicorn, afterwards a griffin and in the end, a human. He was Sam again. His eyes were closed. Then, he vapourised in air. I don't know why a tear got dropped from my left eye. Sam was my best friend. Actually, it hurts very much when a friend betrays you. A friend understands us and remains with us in our needs. All the time spent with Sam flashed before my eyes.

In Indian holy script, *Geeta*, it was written that the *aatma*, or the soul, can never die. No weapon can kill it, no fire can burn it, neither can water make it wet, nor can air carry it away. Soul is eternal. I wished that if Sam reincarnated, he would become a better person. It was very bad that he chose the wrong path. Revenge is very bad. I realised the true meaning of this after Sam's, or Unitaur's death!

When the people are going to die,
Then why are so many relations;
When the world is going to end,
Then why are so many people?
The judgment day will arrive,
We all will bow down,
Before the one,
Who has the key,
To the Chest of Happiness!

□

20

The Journey Ends

We were walking out of the castle. There was no centaur in the corridors. I was still feeling bad for the Unitaur. He should've listened to us and neglected the idea of revenge.

Selira whispered to me, "Who is this unicorn, Parth?"

I told her how I had met Stan in this forest and how he brought me here.

Then, Selira asked to the centaur king, "Why did you return here?"

He answered, "I thought you will need a quick transport. After all, you don't want to face all those difficulties again, do you?"

I remembered something. "Hey, how are Selira's parents?"

Selira's eyes lighted up. The centaur king replied, "Oh, they were so persistent by asking questions about Selira. I told them all about Selira's mission and how she is handling it, but then also they were not satisfied."

"Wait, wait, I just remembered something!" I ran back towards the practicing arena, searched that pile of stones and saw it. Glittering from the inside, the

Unirod was kept there as if it had fought a very fierce battle and was resting afterwards.

I picked it up and then saw those feathers of the Unitaur. They were as big as my elbow. I collected five of them and kept them in my bag. They can be of use in the future-I thought.

Then I ran outside. From the corner of my eye, I saw that dagger which Selira had given me. It was lying under a pile of those feathers. I took it and placed it in the waist belt.

When others saw me with that Unirod, they patted me on the back for defeating that Unitaur and bringing back the lost power of the Uniball.

The centaur king had brought the plane underground somehow. We entered into it. It was completely a modern plane and looked a lot like a spaceship. We flew up and then backwards. Then I saw the place from where he had brought the plane underground. It was a big hole in the ground and was just big enough for a plane to pass.

We were sitting in that plane when Selira said, "Hey, we need to tell all the people of Centauria that the war is over and their leader is dead. They should now give up the aim of conquering Florencia."

"I'll do it!" I said with determination.

The centaur king flew the plane higher. It stopped on the position from where the whole Centauria was visible. The king of centaurs opened the hatch. I shielded my eyes from the sharp rays of the morning sun, and looked down on the people of Centauria.

All the centaurs were looking up at us. I yelled, "All the people of Centauria, your commander, Sam..."

I paused but quickly continued,"... The Unitaur is dead. Here is the proof!" I held out the Unirod for them to see. A surprised and uncertain murmuring spread through the crowd.

"From now on, Centauria will be a part of Florencia." I declared. "Those mountains will no longer trap anyone. I announce your king..." I called out to the centaur king. He came up behind me. "Your king is Clotendrius."

Nobody said anything; they just stood there and watched us. Then I understood everything that was happening. I pointed the Unirod towards them and small threads of blue energy came from each person's mind. All the people of the city fell into a deep sleep.

There was no need to say so much. I explained, "The Unitaur had hypnotised them. The effect is over now. All the people will be awake in some time. They will not remember anything about that Unitaur."

"Thanks for all this, Parth!" He said emotionally. Sunrays had just touched the surface of the earth and already it looked like a new and purified day.

We reached Florencia in thirty minutes. The plane landed on that tall tower where Prime Unicorn lived (the tower was really so big). We came out and saw Prime Unicorn standing there. We all bowed before him.

"Welcome, all our heroes!!" It was good to hear his soothing voice again. He said, "Clotendrius, you are a very good friend of ours. Now you may return. And yes, please turn off those mountains and remove all those beasts and traps. We will need you in future!"

The king bowed again and went back in his plane.

Then, he turned towards Stan, "Stan, you did a great work by bringing Parth here. You should go to the city and tell me all about those new people whom Clotendrius transferred here."

Stan also bowed and went back.

Then he addressed Selira, "Selira, you've done a great work. The whole Florencia will be grateful to you and here is your prize..." His horn glowed and Selira's parents came from behind a door. The moment they saw Selira, they ran towards her and hugged her tightly.

Meanwhile, Prime Unicorn said, "Parth, come with me to the Uni-Chamber."

He went down and I followed him. We entered into the Uni-Chamber. The door got closed behind us.

The Prime Unicorn told me to keep the Unirod near the Uniball, "This was the lost energy which you found!"

The top of the box opened and Uniball absorbed all the energy of that Unirod. The cubicle inside it vanished and it became transparent.

"Where is that stolen energy?" he said.

I took out the pen and kept it near the Uniball. Its crystal got separated and then its energy was absorbed. The crystal again got attached to the pen.

Then he said, "Now tell me the full story of what happened with you on this quest!"

I told him everything that we came across. When I had finished, he said, "Do you have any questions?"

"Sir, can I keep this pen?" I really wanted to keep that pen as it had saved me many times (this was dramatic).

"Yes, yes, it's yours, you can keep it!" he smiled.

"Sir, when we were fighting that Unitaur, my whole hand became a shield even when that pen was not in my hand." I said doubtfully.

"It happened because you had controlled the pen and it knew when you needed help, so it gave you that shield!" he smiled.

"And sir, when Sam..., I mean the Unitaur had trapped me, he said that he had a secret which he had not told anyone. What was that?"

"His first secret was those wings which you had blasted. His second secret was that his whole power was stored in his horn which you broke off. The only way to defeat him was by that horn and you were able to break it. Probably destiny chose you for this task. This was because your soul is very pure. You have a sacred power inside you. No one else can do what you did." I was feeling very special but the things which he told me afterwards were totally unbelievable.

"But why me? I mean, there are hundreds of kids in this world, so why only me?" I was not sure about this.

"There was a great king in Rome called Marcus Oralius. He was also a philosopher. He stated that everything in this world happens because of a reason. Everything is according to the will of god. Coincidences also become important sometimes. It was a coincidence that you are an Indian who is chosen. To make it simpler we can describe it like this:

"In your mythologies, it is written that when the evil rises and becomes powerful, god takes a form or avatar and defeats the evil and establishes peace. After you, somebody else will be chosen and so on. You are not less than an avatar for us. Yes, you are an avatar for us!"

After hearing this, I was sure that the Prime Unicorn was mistaken somewhere. "But, I cannot be that avatar. I have no special powers, and I am definitely no god!"

"You are not a god; you are a piece of that god! You are only a spark of that powerful fire that burns in the court of god. And you don't need any special powers to become an avatar. You already have a power, the power of courage, love and trust. You are only a small piece of this whole world. Everything in this world changes and gets destroyed when its time arrives."

He continued, "When you came to Rome, the Uniball told me that the person has arrived who will save us. He will have a clean heart and he will never step back from problems. And probably that is why the Uniball's energy took the form of a pen. It wanted itself to be discovered by you!"

It was good that there was a table kept behind me as I had to take the support of that table to stand. It was difficult to believe the Prime Unicorn.

"But I have many problems in mathematics and I don't want to do it!" I said.

He started laughing. He laughed for a minute and then said, "Mathematical problems can also be solved if you don't step back from them."

I sighed, "Then in that matter, no power in this world can help me."

Then I remembered something and said, "Why was Selira chosen? Is she also some kind of avatar?"

"She was chosen because she was born for a purpose. Her birth was not an ordinary one! She was born at a time when all the planets of the universe were in a similar pattern. That time is a very precious one. If she chose the wrong path, then no one, even you, would be able to stop her."

"The Unitaur helped us without knowing it. He trapped her parents so she was determined to bring them back. Her grandfather knew that she was no ordinary girl. So, he gave her the training and taught her to use all the weapons."

"When you came here, the Uniball told me that the boy has arrived and he will be alone here. Then I told Stan to keep an eye on you and you turned out to be the special one."

"Sir, how was the Unitaur able to steal the power of Uniball? He told me that he did it by cutting off the horns of five powerful unicorns. Who were they?" I asked out of curiosity.

"Those five unicorns were the previous Prime Unicorns. There is a ritual in Florencia. No unicorn ever dies. When they become old, they give themselves to the Uniball. But this is not the case with the Prime Unicorns. When a Prime Unicorn is not able to guard the Uniball, the Uniball gives him a new form and they go in the outer world to live as adults. In their human old age, they again return and share their knowledge with us and the Uniball. The five former Prime Unicorns mysteriously disappeared, probably abducted by the Unitaur. Then, as you know, he used their horns to steal Uniball's power." He finished.

"But why did the Uniball let him steal that power?" I questioned.

"The Uniball trusts the Prime Unicorns completely. When that Unitaur used those horns, the Uniball probably got confused and gave its power." He Explained.

I nodded, but another doubt entered my mind. "Okay, but wait a second!! That Unitaur couldn't have thought this plan by himself!"

"Why do you think so?"

"When I tried to talk to him, he gave me a lot of information without ever thinking about what he was saying. So he cannot plan all that, "I added after a pause, "According to me."

"You are correct. This plan was thought by someone else. I'll tell you from the starting. Three unicorns are chosen for the position of Prime Unicorn and the Uniball chooses one from them. After I was chosen, the Unitaur became very angry and decided to steal the Uniball's power. He manipulated the third candidate to help him in his work. This third candidate had a very intelligent mind. He possibly suggested this plan. When they went to steal the Uniball's power for the first time, the Uniball understood their intentions and punished them. You know what happened to the Unitaur. He probably refined the technique and succeeded in stealing the Uniball's energy." The Prime Unicorn completed.

"But what happened to that third unicorn?" I asked again.

"I don't know. He went into hiding. Some say he died and some think he is still hiding and planning to attack Florencia."

"What do you think?"

"I don't know." He repeated. "But if he returns, we will need you again!" He smiled.

I was sad that I had to leave Florencia but the thought of coming back here lighted me up. Obviously I didn't want any harm of Florencia but wanted to come here often.

I asked the question which I was longing to ask. "Will I come here in the future? I mean without any cause."

"Everything has a cause Parth, but we will need you soon. Now, you should return to your world. You may say goodbye to your friend!" He nodded.

I bowed before him. Then, I picked up that pen and went upstairs. Selira's parents were talking with her. When I went there she said to her dad, "You go, I'll come in a second!"

Her parents went to those stairs and climbed down. I said, "Selira, I am going back. So, goodbye! You were a very good and courageous companion!"

She said nothing and hugged me tightly. Then, she said, "I will miss you a lot, Parth! Please return soon. Goodbye!" Then she suddenly kissed me on the cheek and ran towards the stairs. She looked back one last time and waved her hand before disappearing down the stairs.

I was standing there. I could feel my whole face becoming red. At the same time, there was a mixed feeling of joy and sadness. Then Prime Unicorn came there and said, "Parth, now you should go. Goodbye! And yes, I have a gift for you, "He gave me a small book. "Read it and your math problems will be solved."

"Really???" I was very happy.

"Yes really, but you yourself will have to concentrate on it. Math only wants concentration."

His horn glowed and a doorway appeared on the edge of that tower. It looked just like the door which he had made when my journey began. I stepped through the door and closed my eyes. When I opened them, I was standing between trees and plants. My bicycle was fallen near my feet. All my cuts, bruises and wounds had disappeared but I still felt tired.

I took it and pedaled very fast to Mr. Clapperton's house. In the way, I hoped to see Sam's house and he sitting in the veranda. But, his house was replaced by the house which was ahead of it.

I rang the bell of Mr. Clapperton's house. He came out, saw me and quickly took me inside before closing the door.

I said, "We defeated the Unitaur. The Uniball is complete now."

"Good job! I was not sure if you could do it! Now, when you were gone, I regularly kept changing the duration of the days to minutes. You were in Florencia for thirteen days and I changed each of them into minutes. Now, you can go back to your farmhouse."

"But I told my aunt that I will be going to the countryside. If I go back so soon, she would get suspicious!"

"Then you can wait here for some time. In that time, you can tell me your full adventures. I'll make some coffee for both of us!"

So, we had coffee and I told him about the journey. I was feeling extremely excited while telling him all that.

After hearing the story, he said, "Great, you did a courageous work and I would definitely like to meet this girl Selira. Really, love, trust and courage combine and give a person his super powers."

I nodded and took a sip of the hot coffee. He said, "Now, you should have a bath."

I took his advice and really, it felt better to some extent! Now I felt much better.

I spent one hour there and I learned that Mr. Clapperton was a very good man. He was friendly and trustful. I left his house and went to my house.

I remembered that whenever I heard that there was a war between countries, I felt very bad. I also remembered that whenever I saw a small kid being bullied, I always went to save him. I was also not feeling well when I came in Rome. That must have been because the Unitaur was becoming powerful and Uniball's power was stolen.

I reached to my farmhouse, parked the cycle and went in.

When my uncle saw me, he said, "Hey Parth, I learned that you went to the countryside. So, how was the experience?"

"Um…It was good. I enjoyed a lot with my friends. I'm having a headache, so I'm going to my room!" I ran upstairs.

Behind me, aunt Kshama came out of the kitchen and I heard them talk, "What happened to him?"

"I don't know! He said he is having a headache!" Uncle Dhairya said.

I came in my room and lied down on the bed. I started thinking about the adventures which I had in Florencia and above all, Selira! She was a true friend and I really trusted her. While thinking all that, I went into a deep sleep.

□

Epilogue

Parth woke up. He remembered the adventures that he had in Florencia. Was it a dream? – He wondered. He jumped off the bed and picked up his backpack. It was empty. Then he opened his wardrobe and searched for his jacket, but it was also not there. He quickly ran downstairs.

His uncle and aunt wished him 'good morning' but he said, "Aunt, do you know where is my jacket which I wore yesterday?"

"Which jacket?" Aunt Kshama asked.

"The one which..." he stopped and ran outside. His uncle and aunt were puzzled. In the way, he saw the calendar. Today was his last day in Rome. He reached to his bicycle and observed it completely. There was nothing wrong with it.

He looked over to the other houses but Mr. Clapperton's dark and gloomy house was nowhere to be seen. He wondered again – Was it all really a dream?

"Whether it was or not, it was truly exciting!" He said to himself and stretched his gaze over to the horizon. The sun was rising and its golden rays were refreshing everything.

He thought – Today is my last day in Rome and I don't know whether I will be returning or not, but I will take back with me such delightful memories of this place that I will never forget. Good bye Rome, Good bye!!!

❋❋❋

Parth was in the plane. Rome was left behind and the plane was flying towards India. He was thinking about his parents, but was not able to forget that adventurous dream. He decided to write it all in his diary. So, he took out his diary and searched for a pen. He found one in the left pocket of his jeans. He took it out and looked at it.

It was the same pen which he had seen in his dream!!! The same one!! Its small blue crystal was shining faintly on top of it!!

□□□